Communities, Churches and Social Capital in Northern Ireland

Derek Bacon

Centre for Voluntary Action Studies

University of Ulster

Communities, Churches and Social Capital in Northern Ireland

ISBN 1 85923 176 4

© 2003, the author

This publication has received financial support from the Community Relations Council which aims to enable change towards a society free from sectarianism.

Page layout and design by Zing Design and Print, Coleraine, N. Ireland   e-mail design@zingdp.com

Photo credit: Copyright of the cover photograph of this book is hereby acknowledged as the property of DeskPicture.com

The Centre for Voluntary Action Studies is a research centre in the Faculty of Social Sciences at the University of Ulster. It exists to promote, develop and conduct research on voluntary action both as a contribution to international scholarship and as a resource for the development of the voluntary sector in Northern Ireland and further afield.

Centre for Voluntary Action Studies
University of Ulster
Coleraine, BT52 1SA
Northern Ireland

Tel: 028 7032 4865
http://www.ulst.ac.uk/cvas/

CONTENTS

ACKNOWLEDGEMENTS 6

PREFACE 7

TERMS OF REFERENCE 8

EXECUTIVE SUMMARY 9

SECTION 1 *CONTEXT* 20

The religious background 20
Third way politics and the appeal of social capital 22
The policy climate and faith-based organisations 24
Why this project? 27

SECTION 2 *PROJECT DESIGN AND IMPLEMENTATION* 30

Aims and objectives 30
Research design 31
Sampling issues 32
Negotiating access 34
Interview schedule and survey questionnaire 35

SECTION 3 *PROFILES OF TWELVE FAITH-BASED ORGANISATIONS* 36

Catholic
Charitable trust: Flax Trust Limited, Belfast 37
Parish: Holy Family, Belfast 40
Company: Boys and Girls Club, Omagh 43

Presbyterian
Congregation: Ballysillan, Belfast 45
Congregation: 'Benmoe', 'Ballycarn' 48

	Church of Ireland	
	Parish: Knocknagoney, Belfast	50
	Parish: Shankill, Lurgan	52
	Methodist	
	Congregation: City Mission, Londonderry	56
	Trust: Barnabas Trust, Enniskillen	58
	Cross-denominational	
	Association: YMCA (National Council), Belfast	60
	New Church	
	Company: Oasis Care, Belfast	63
	Unaffiliated	
	Company: Mornington Community Project, Belfast	65
SECTION 4	**CASE STUDIES OF FIVE FAITH-BASED ORGANISATIONS**	68
	'Benmoe's' 'Shebeg' Pastoral Centre, 'Ballycarn'	68
	Shankill's Jethro Project, Lurgan	76
	Holy Family Catholic Parish, Belfast	80
	Oasis Family Centre, Belfast	84
	Mornington Community Project, Belfast	91
SECTION 5	**THE SURVEY**	96
	Survey purpose, distribution and response rate	96
	Survey analysis	97
	Profile of the sample	98
	The local community and respondents' relation to it	100
	Reciprocity and local trust	105
	Voluntary action, broader participation and civic engagement	108
	Religious behaviour	110
	Personal attitudes, values and beliefs	112
	People and networks	117
	Social capital infrastructure	118
	Summing up	119

SECTION 6	***FINDINGS***	120
	What churches and para-churches are doing	121
	Activities by broad area	122
	Activities by social capital domain	123
	Who benefits and how	126
	Cross-community benefit	129
	Community cohesion and social capital formation	133
	Leadership, funding and fragility	138
SECTION 7	***DISCUSSION AND CONCLUSIONS***	145
	Key findings	145
	Churches and commitment, risk and trust	148
	Social capital and religious values	151
	Bringing together policy, practice and research	155
	Some recommendations	157

APPENDICES

	I *Notes on social capital*	161
	II *Rationale for the amended project design*	168
	III *The semi-structured interview schedule*	170
	IV *The survey questionnaire*	172

REFERENCES 194

ACKNOWLEDGEMENTS

I salute first the people from the churches and other organisations described in this report. They gave willingly of their time and shared their insights.

I thank the project funding bodies for their financial contributions: The Northern Ireland Educational Foundation; The Derwent Trust; The Centre for Voluntary Action Studies and The Community Relations Council. They made the work and its publication possible.

I mark my gratitude to some key informants in both church and academic life with a wide knowledge of the Northern Ireland scene. They pointed to suggestive avenues of exploration.

I offer my thanks to the advisory group, Dr Margaret Harris and Dr Helen Cameron in Britain and Dr Ram Cnaan and Dr Bob Wineburg in the United States. They supplied valuable critical input that was always welcome, though not always incorporated.

Academic colleagues at home and abroad provided interest and ready comment. The members of the project team, Dr Arthur Williamson and Dr Kerry O'Halloran, were crucial to the direction of the research. The change of method, the misperceptions and other infelicities are my responsibility alone.

Derek Bacon
Autumn 2003

PREFACE

People just didn't know about resources in the church for the community,
Minister, 'Benmoe' congregation.

In the final decade of the twentieth century the public benefit work of churches began to come under growing scrutiny in the world of international Third Sector research. This accompanied a policy debate in the United States, in the United Kingdom and in other countries where the boundaries of state welfare provision were under review.

The debate continues and is now informed by a growing body of empirical studies into the strengths and weaknesses of faith-based voluntary action. It reflects a new awareness of the role that religious organisations have traditionally played in dealing with social need in local communities. It centres on moves to encourage greater contemporary involvement of churches and faith-based organisations in a range of community benefit programmes through initiatives to broaden the access of such organisations to government support.

In Northern Ireland, where it is far from clear whether religion is more truly to be regarded as a source of community division or community cohesion, questions raised within the debate about public support for religious organisations have a particular force. Sooner or later may come the necessity to implement policy initiatives in relation to social inclusion, similar to those in Britain, that openly invite participation by local faith communities in the work of neighbourhood regeneration. This presents a dilemma because, while there is perhaps a broad awareness of a social action dimension to churches in the province, policy-makers have little or no detailed knowledge of the contribution that churches and other faith-based organisations make to meeting social need or to community development. Nor do they have a clear grasp of what might be expected of such bodies.

This report identifies and assesses the public benefit work of 12 churches and other faith-based organisations in Northern Ireland that both respond to human need and contribute to the building of a more inclusive society. In doing so it demonstrates that further and fuller investigation into the impact of faith-based organisations is imperative.

TERMS OF REFERENCE

Two broad aims, set out in the original proposal submitted to the funding body, are at the heart of this research project.

The first:
> 'to identify examples of church-related voluntary action which offer potential for the social capital formation necessary to promote church and community coordination of social resources in addressing community issues'.

The second:
> 'to produce data and analyses which will increase understanding of the relationships between churches and their respective communities in Northern Ireland'.

These aims are broken down into four objectives.

1. To add to existing knowledge and understanding of the role of the churches in their respective communities in Northern Ireland; in particular with regard to their work in providing welfare services and facilities and, specifically, in generating bridging social capital.

2. To provide empirical data which identifies, measures and differentiates the exercise of that role in different communities.

3. To identify trends, assess quality and enhance knowledge and understanding of community-related church activities that are demonstrably beneficial.

4. To explore the relevance of concepts such as 'leadership', 'sustaining community cohesion', 'cross-community benefit' in the context of the church/community relationship.

EXECUTIVE SUMMARY

KEY PURPOSES OF THE RESEARCH

The central purpose of this research project was to gather information about the voluntary activity that is carried out by and through a range of churches and other faith-based organisations ('FBOs') across Northern Ireland, to read this activity in social capital terms and to begin to assess its value to society.

There is perhaps a general awareness of a social action dimension to churches, but no details of the scope and nature of the work carried out through church-related voluntary action are available to Northern Ireland's Voluntary and Community Unit of the Department of Social Development. Hence this project, by providing illustrative information, aimed to highlight the existing deficit and underline the need for further research to aid policy development in line with central government neighbourhood regeneration and social inclusion initiatives.

METHODS

Field work examining voluntary action in church and para-church organisations was carried out in Belfast, Derry, Enniskillen, Lurgan, Omagh and one other provincial town ('Ballycarn') through 2001 and into 2002. In an investigation of 12 FBOs, 46 semi-structured interviews were carried out and 88 responses to a survey questionnaire were obtained, a response rate of 73.3 percent.

THE REPORT

Section 1 sets the context by noting the place, reach and polarised condition of the churches in Northern Ireland. It introduces the concept of social capital that underpins the New Labour project and highlights its impact upon the policy climate, tracing new central government sensitivity to the potential of faith groups to contribute to the wellbeing of local communities. Turning to the contemporary enthusiasm for strategic partnerships that engage faith communities in neighbourhood regeneration initiatives, it considers the questions surrounding any extension of a similar policy to this corner of the United Kingdom. Drawing attention to the body of empirical evidence about the public benefit work of churches that is available from recent international third sector research, it sets the scene for the search for evidence of any similar activity by churches in Northern Ireland.

Section 2 provides information about the initial research design and methodology employed for meeting the aims of the project.

Section 3 presents profiles of the twelve organisations, built up from the interviews, under the following headings: Type, Objectives, Activities, Buildings, Participation, Resourcing and Use of Research, Linkages and Cross-Community Dimension.

Section 4 sets out five case studies which, in trying to communicate something of the flavour and 'feel' of some aspects of what are very different organisations, follow a less uniform style than that of the profiles.

Section 5 lays out information produced by the 88 returns from the survey, examines the main findings and presents some characteristics of the people who are engaged in the work of the organisations profiled in the study.

Section 6 presents findings from the interviews on what churches and para-churches are doing. These follow below, categorised first by broad area, then under social capital domains.

ACTIVITIES BY BROAD AREA

Community support programmes
Projects offer help in the sphere of community development, tackling crime, environmental issues, traffic calming, home safety and energy. They include community cafés and shops, playgroups and after school care, family support and meals on wheels. There are opportunities for art, drama and sport for all ages and abilities.

Health programmes
Projects range from services for people with mental illness to physically disabled people. They cover divorce, bereavement, respite for carers, women's issues, support for single parents and for senior citizens. Advice and counselling are available to people with problems relating to alcohol or other substance abuse.

Social programmes
Youth projects facilitate personal and social development for young people. Drop-in centres disseminate and exchange information and advice on welfare, housing and other problems. Accommodation is provided in hostels for homeless people or in newly built housing units. Emergency shelter and assistance with immediate needs are made available. Credit unions are in operation.

Educational programmes
Lifelong learning opportunities are provided and promoted. People with learning difficulties are encouraged and supported. There are parenting courses and homework clubs. Study groups address community reconciliation and social justice issues. Experiential learning opportunities are offered to volunteers.

Training programmes
IT training into jobs is provided, often for people on the margins of society, as part of what is in some cases an integrated strategy of economic regeneration.

ACTIVITIES BY SOCIAL CAPITAL DOMAIN

The significance of the church-related voluntary activities discovered through this project comes sharply into relief when they are summarised and categorised under the eight domains of social capital drawn from the work of Forrest and Kearns (Forrest and Kearns, 2001).

Empowerment
Amongst the twelve organisations studied are those:

- enlarging the range of channels for the empowerment of citizens, encouraging them to be more community-oriented, cooperative and participative in ways that range from carrying out a community audit to involvement in management of church owned resources;

- providing access to ICT in order to connect individuals and strengthen community knowledge and sharing;
- developing locally appropriate programmes in support of welfare to work transitions and career guidance;
- channelling potential for credentialled educational attainment and jobs by alternative routes through education, business or community links;
- providing training and experience for parents in support of families, making parenting a more collective activity and enabling them to expand their social networks, often across the community divide;
- facilitating local business incubation and retail outlets.

Participation
Amongst the twelve organisations studied are those:

- strengthening actual and potential young offenders' positive social capital and raising their ambition through employment or volunteer placement;
- releasing and fostering artistic and creative gifts and providing a platform for their expression and celebration in the public space.

Associational activity and common purpose
Amongst the twelve organisations studied are those:

- facilitating lifelong learning, adult study groups, forums and circles, which include the work of peacebuilding and reconciliation across the community divide;
- ensuring the availability of primary health care and associated services.

Supporting networks and reciprocity
Amongst the twelve organisations studied are those:

- contributing to partnerships with other agencies working for community revitalisation and bringing national and international resources to bear on local issues;
- widening opportunities for young people to work alongside people from different social and ethnic backgrounds away from the home situation;
- setting up networks of street representatives.

Collective norms and values
Amongst the twelve organisations studied are those:

- building local pride and rootedness and a sense of responsibility for, and ownership of, the quality of community life;

Executive Summary 13

- promoting norms and values that discourage criminal behaviour in at risk young people.

Trust
Amongst the twelve organisations studied are those:

- extending potential for the loving relationships that stimulate children's physical, intellectual and emotional growth and positively influence their capacity to build trusting social relationships in later life;
- offering personal relationships that enhance the self-worth of young people through relationally based youth work and mentoring;
- reducing social distance and fostering inter-personal trust.

Safety
Amongst the twelve organisations studied are those:

- making housing available;
- giving information and advice, food, financial assistance, temporary and long-term shelter, clothing, refuge from domestic violence;
- supporting those who are bereaved and those who have been traumatised;
- encouraging home safety and energy conservation schemes.

Belonging
Amongst the twelve organisations studied are those:

- breaking down a sense of isolation amongst older people and actively addressing threats to mental health;
- creating opportunities for young people in service learning and community volunteering;
- bringing the tangible assistance and care that begin to recreate a sense of well being and belonging to those who are socially excluded - disabled people, long-term unemployed people, those with criminal convictions, those suffering drug or alcohol abuse, those who are temporarily homeless;
- engaging in environmental improvement projects.

The churches and para-churches which are the subject of this report are deeply engaged in voluntary activities that enable people to build a sense of growing as a community within areas of deprivation and social exclusion in Northern Ireland. Their voluntary activities are producing outcomes in line with those noted in the *Partners for Change* document of the Northern Ireland Department of Social Development (DSD, 2001). Those outcomes include:

- increased employability;
- greater attention to equality issues;
- the acquisition of new skills;
- increased community safety;
- a more supportive environment for children and young people;
- better community relations within and between communities;
- environmental improvement;
- developing community infrastructure in areas where it is weak.

The spectrum of voluntary activity in which these organisations are engaged goes beyond traditional services for church members. It takes in building local rootedness and pride in community life. It includes enlarging channels for the empowerment of all citizens and contributing to partnerships with other agencies working for community revitalisation. The social capital that they generate in the course of their spiritual and practical activities is embedded in networks that have a presence in every community on the island of Ireland with well developed cross border national structures as well as extensive international links. They have leaders who live in the community they serve; they have a range of specialists upon whom they may call and they have their own financial resources. With their values driving a concern for issues that government has a duty to address, they comprise significant networks and key sources of social capital.

Section 7 provides a discussion that acknowledges the limited capacity of churches to make much impact upon the huge forces at work in society in Northern Ireland. It points nevertheless to evidence of a commitment within these faith communities that stems from, and builds upon, religious values, is willing to take risks, fosters a positive and people-centred approach to regeneration and drives a dynamic that encourages social capital formation. Having demonstrated that church-related voluntary action is of benefit not just to church members, but to the well being of society at large, the report concludes by insisting that a job remains to be done on breaking down misperceptions of churches and that further research into this dimension of their work in Northern Ireland is imperative.

Executive Summary 15

KEY FINDINGS

Type of faith-based organisation
From small congregations to large para-churches, faith-based organisations (FBOs) are to be found in a striking range of forms and types in Northern Ireland. They are usually embedded in the community and not staffed and administered from outside as are statutory agencies.

Objectives
The objectives of churches and other FBOs are variously expressed but usually involve an intent to change human lives and conditions for the better. They exhibit value commitments that are of enormous social significance.

Activities
A huge diversity of activities, services and facilities is made available through churches and FBOs both for members and for people outside the membership circle. By such means these organisations form and sustain significant reserves of social capital that are available to the local community.

Buildings
The premises used by churches and FBOs are often important sites for civic engagement in local communities.

Participation
Programmes run by churches and FBOs are supported by large numbers of volunteers, of whom many see such voluntary activity as a practical expression of their faith. The spiritual dimension of the organisation provides an underpinning to the practical work. The faith base adds urgency to social commitment and plays a large part in motivating the 2000 volunteers at work in the 12 organisations investigated in this project.

Resourcing and use of research
The churches and FBOs examined here have considerable financial, human and physical resources. They need a greater appreciation of the value of research in enabling the most effective and efficient use of their resources.

Linkages
There is evidence that churches and FBOs may be opening up to a greater awareness of the value of working cooperatively and in partnership with other

bodies. Some unexpected and positive collaborative relationships are in place through their bridging and linking social capital. Where shared concern leads to united local effort by churches, denominational boundaries are becoming less significant.

Cross-community dimension
There is universal recognition of the importance of this dimension in the context of Northern Ireland and some courageous steps have been taken by the churches and FBOs in the study. They serve to highlight the need for further imaginative action to contribute towards wider social cohesion. Three quarters of the survey respondents said that the churches should be doing much more to improve community relations.

Flexibility
These organisations demonstrate considerable flexibility and imagination in their responses to local conditions. However all responses seem to have begun from a deliberate attempt to look carefully at, and identify with, the local community, to listen to local expression of need and to decide how best to stimulate local action to address that need. In some cases this is by direct provision of services or facilities. In some it is by facilitating provision by other agencies.

Social inclusion and social cohesion
These organisations are making serious attempts to reach the most marginalised and vulnerable people in local communities. They are doing so in a way that both contributes to an improvement in people's material conditions and nurtures the heart of the community.

Dissolving stereotypes
The case studies present a picture of organisations that have moved beyond the received view of the churches as representatives of ethnic loyalty and markers of separatist communities. Complementing these findings are the responses from the survey which show members of the organisations as people who have a strong sense of belonging to their church and are often active in other local organisations. They are themselves more concerned to respond to people in need than to add to their church's membership. They want the church to be a compassionate community partner, to care for human wellbeing and to assist neighbourhood development.

Leadership
The quality of leadership in each church or FBO is crucial for shaping the direction, strength and sustainability of its voluntary engagement.

Executive Summary

SOME RECOMMENDATIONS

To churches

- Churches have enormous theological resources to shape a social vision that would enhance the reach of current government policy. They should take confidence in this fact and, from a position of cooperation with sister churches, collaboration with public and statutory bodies and solidarity with socially excluded people, they should actively look for ways to contribute to the making of social policy.

- Churches should examine their theological resources and open themselves to a renewed understanding of their embeddedness in local communities and of their acts of public worship as socially significant expressions of inclusion and social capital formation.

- Churches have trained leaders who are often people of vision and commitment. They should review their programmes of training and consider including modules that build upon their leaders' strengths to promote an enabling and facilitating approach to ministry. The United Reformed Church module on church-related community work for its ministers provides one example of good practice.

- Churches have large human capital resources. They should more actively and systematically encourage their people to see the volunteering of their time, energy and expertise to the well being of the local community as a vital expression of faith.

- Churches possess significant physical resources in terms of buildings in key locations. They should look again at the totality of the resources represented by their faith, their people and their premises and seek ways of using them to build community morale, cooperation and confidence.

- Churches know the value of networks. They should more wholeheartedly grasp the opportunities that are available to them within voluntary sector networks of communication and support and should further benefit their local communities through the use of the bridging and linking social capital from their wider contacts.

- Churches should become more sensitive to the limited effectiveness of working in isolation and should add value to their social action by collaborating with other agencies in the work of building social cohesion and developing stable local communities.

- Churches can create encounters between people who would otherwise never meet, crossing divisions of gender, age and class. They should build into their local strategy a community project dimension that would give practical expression to this inclusive dimension to their faith. This might take service provision form or, for example, an exercise to monitor the impact of specific social policies upon socially excluded groups in the neighbourhood.

- Churches should become more aware of the importance of research and evaluation for the provision of ready examples of good practice. These examples could be widely shared in a way that would both encourage the mission of the churches and command the attention of policy-makers and inform their decisions.

- Churches should do more to raise the public profile of the nature, range and scale of their deep-rooted commitment to the wellbeing of society in Northern Ireland and should combat public ignorance of their activities or misconceptions about their purposes that are rooted in historical legacy.

- Churches should develop closer contacts with local authorities, support their attempts to serve all of the people within their boundaries and commit to partnerships in local regeneration initiatives.

- Churches should more enthusiastically exploit the opportunities offered by church forums, where they exist, as means of bringing together diverse people and outlooks, for dissemination of information and as instruments of united action.

- Churches should support and benefit from the skills and expertise of an existing umbrella body like the Churches Community Work Alliance for training and for information about practice and about funding streams.

To policy-makers

- Policy-makers appear to have a limited perception of churches and other faith-based organisations. They should invest energy, resources and time in uncovering how these bodies encounter and minister to people in the context of their whole life experience, offering different types of social capital that are important at different times over an individual's lifetime. They should also make themselves aware of the work of such bodies towards transformation and regeneration at many levels from the spiritual to the political.

- Policy-makers should seek out and renew the channels of communication with the churches and fully appraise them, at local as well as central level, of the thrust and direction of contemporary policy. They should invite the participation of the churches in meeting policy objectives that are in line with their mission and in a way that encourages them to share information, understand and support each other and work together.

- Bearing in mind the way in which churches already cooperate with local authorities elsewhere in the UK and recognising the signs of a growing willingness to work collaboratively in Northern Ireland, policy-makers should facilitate the participation of churches by enabling the production and widespread dissemination of Northern Ireland versions of training and information publications already in use in Britain. The DETR and LGA manuals provide good examples (Randolph-Horn, 2000; LGA, 2002).

- Policy-makers should take steps to ensure that orientation and awareness training opportunities are put in place for government officers engaging with churches and, where these do not exist, consider appointing liaison or development officers to facilitate the process of dialogue and discovery.

- Policy-makers should provide clear information about funding streams and, with appropriate safeguards, make such funding more readily accessible.

SECTION 1   CONTEXT

The section opens by noting the place, reach and polarised condition of the churches in Northern Ireland. It introduces the concept of social capital that underpins the New Labour project and highlights its impact upon the policy climate, tracing new central government sensitivity to the potential of faith groups to contribute to the wellbeing of local communities. Turning to the contemporary enthusiasm for strategic partnerships that engage faith communities in neighbourhood regeneration initiatives, it considers the questions surrounding any extension of a similar policy to this part of the United Kingdom. The section draws attention to the substantial body of empirical evidence about the public benefit work of churches that is available from recent international third sector research and it sets the scene for the search for evidence of any similar activity by churches in Northern Ireland.

THE RELIGIOUS BACKGROUND

Research suggests that in Northern Ireland nine out of ten people identify themselves as belonging to a church (Brewer, 2002). With latest figures showing the population approaching 1.7 million (NISRA, 2001), this implies that there may be over 1,530,000 people with some kind of church link. The 2001 Northern Ireland Census Religion figures are given below.

Table 1. Northern Ireland Census 2001 Religion

Religion	Number	Percentage (unadjusted)
Roman Catholic	678,462	40.26
Presbyterian	348,742	20.69
Church of Ireland	257,788	15.30
Methodist	59,173	3.51
Other denominations	102,221	6.07
Other religions	5,028	0.30
None or not stated	233,853	13.87
All Persons	1,685,267	100.0

These raw figures show roughly 86 percent of a total population of 1,685,267 people claiming an attachment to a Christian church and a further 0.30 percent indicating affiliation with another religion. When adjustment for the community background question in the census is made, the official figure given for religious affiliation in the province is 96.89 percent Christian, 0.39 percent other religions and philosophies and 2.72 percent who cannot be allocated. Statistics from the various churches tend to show membership figures lower than those in the census (See Richardson, 1998), but it is nevertheless clear that religion in Northern Ireland has a major place in society. The churches touch deep roots in everyday human life and the level and range of their voluntary welfare activity in response to social need in the community has been found to be extensive and important (Bacon, 1998; Hamilton, 2002; Harrison, 2000; Morrow, 1995).

Despite this positive side to their activity, the churches are more generally viewed and discussed in the news media as part of the problem of Northern Ireland rather than as a source of healing and community building. Further, if the general sense of *The Believers' Enquiry* (Kenny, 1998) is accurate, churches in Northern Ireland are not driven by any urgency to reach out to each other, let alone to reach out together in response to social need. The findings of research by Liechty and Clegg (2001) for the Irish School of Ecumenics and by Williamson et al. (2001) for the Community Relations Council could strengthen the impression that most churches secretly wish to be left alone with the form of 'comfortable apartheid' they have inherited, separated from each other within their own communities.

One observer of religion in Northern Ireland makes a darker point, contending that, in its concrete church form, religion 'solidifies the opposing alliances in an exclusive way and precludes a common state form, thus providing the structure of violence which such divisions entail' (Fulton, 1991 p.131). The opposing alliances that matter are political ones. But these competing traditions of Nationalism and Unionism are bound up with cultural identities for which religious belonging has great significance and into which religious belief and attitude are incorporated. Not all Catholics are Nationalists, but 63 percent of them describe themselves as such. Not all Protestants are Unionists, but 74 percent of them say they are (NI Life and Times, 1998). The two distinct communities, each commonly designated by a religious tag, compete for space and power. Thus political interactions are never totally free from association with religion and inter-church relationships come to be understood to have a political significance beyond the churches themselves.

These Catholic and Protestant communities have, for generations, been assembling their own social service infrastructure, centred often on their churches. Through the nineteenth century increasing religious polarisation in the north of Ireland ensured the emergence of parallel structures of benevolence accompanied by the beginning of a religiously segregated pattern of housing in a rapidly expanding Belfast (Williamson, 1995). Today some 63 percent of that city's population lives in enclaves that are more than 90 percent Protestant or Catholic. This division is mirrored in many other towns across Northern Ireland and tensions at some interface areas show no signs of dissipating. In such an arena,

> *within the political infrastructure of a divided society, where, by definition, there is more than one single community, more than one single set of politico-cultural values, people may be so interested in their community, their society, that they become willing to kill those within the other, whom they perceive to be threatening or antagonistic to their political, social or economic position* (Cochrane, 2002).

This is the scenario in which the Christian faith communities of Northern Ireland are deeply implicated. So when the Home Secretary asks at Westminster, 'How can we draw on the strength of faith communities for the revitalisation of civil society?' (Blunkett, 2001) he poses a question that is of considerable complexity when applied to this corner of the UK. This is a place where strengthening community cohesion, supporting associational life and fostering a sense of civic responsibility have wider ramifications. Joining a voluntary organisation, building a strong sense of community can have a wholly different meaning and outcome when amongst the most powerful constituents of civil society are paramilitary groups. It is unpromising ground for the seeds of central government 'third way' aspirations to take root.

THIRD WAY POLITICS AND THE APPEAL OF SOCIAL CAPITAL

> *The third way was always intended to renew and modernise progressive politics, not find a soggy compromise between left and right. Ideas are the key; and the tide of ideas is flowing in our direction* (Blair, 2001b).

Section 1 Context   23

One of the currents in that tide of intellectual life claimed for Labour in the same article was cutting-edge work in the social sciences - 'about the nature, limits and dynamics of cooperation, about trust and social capital, knowledge and human capital'. As Marilyn Taylor observes, we can learn a great deal about government policy from the language that it promotes. A language of community is in evidence here. It emphasises the need to invest in social capital as well as in the human and financial capital that dominated past regeneration agendas (Taylor, 2002).

The concept of social capital that underlies much of the New Labour project (Halpern, 1999; Szreter, 2000) is not new. In the contemporary global academic and policy debate there is no single agreed definition of social capital, no universal model of its formation or means of measurement. It has been identified with such features of social organisations as trust, considered as an aggregate of behavioural norms, viewed as social networks, or thought of as a combination of all of these. It has meant different things within different disciplines, usually things that are desirable, cared for and approved of (Dasgupta & Serageldin, 2000). This may be part of its political appeal, so that when a Prime Minister describes it as a 'capacity to get things done, to cooperate' (Blair, 1999), he can mean almost anything.

The Working Papers from the World Bank Initiative on Social Capital describe projects around the globe whose findings suggest that it is an important element in the health, safety, education, political participation and quality of life of poor communities (World Bank, 2002). A recent OECD report includes improved child welfare, lower rates of child abuse and greater general happiness in the range of benefits to individuals and societies accruing from social capital (Cote and Healy, 2001). Those who follow Robert Putnam's approach argue that social capital is vital for the health of civil society and indeed for democracy itself (Putnam, 1995, 2000). Frances Fukuyama sees it as a crucial element in economic development, because increased trust and lower transaction costs make the functioning of the economy more efficient (Fukuyama, 1995). It is linked in the literature to lower crime rates (Halpern, 1999), better health (Wilkinson, 1996) and much else. Michael Woolcock sums it up memorably when he observes that the well connected are more likely to be 'housed, healthy, hired and happy' (Woolcock, 2000).

Of the three major figures associated with the re-emergence and development of the concept, Pierre Bourdieu, James Coleman and Robert Putnam (See Appendix I), it is the last who has caught the popular imagination and given social capital the aura of a public good with accompanying policy relevance and appeal. His claim that social capital is key to understanding civic engagement and to building civil society (Putnam, 1993, 2000) stimulated controversy far beyond the borders of the United States. His definition is deceptively succinct: 'features of social life - networks, norms, and trust - that enable participants to act together more effectively to pursue shared objectives' (Putnam, 1996).

Three types of social capital are distinguished in the literature. 'Bonding' social capital is characterised by strong bonds like those between family members or members of an ethnic group. 'Bridging' social capital designates weaker, less dense but more cross-cutting ties like those between business associates, acquaintances, friends from different ethnic groups. 'Linking' social capital (Woolcock, 2000) refers to connections between people at different levels of power or social status. The capacity of individuals and communities (say, the general public) to access resources, ideas and information from formal institutions beyond the immediate community radius (say, the political elite) could be said to depend upon 'linking' social capital.

To the important differences between types of social capital may be added the distinction between social capital as a 'public good' and as a 'club good'. Social capital is shared by a group, or by groups of individuals. To the extent that all members of society or a community have access, it may constitute a 'public good'. Where groups of individuals can control access by other individuals, it may be more in the nature of a 'club good' and a force for exclusion. Thus, social capital is not without its downside (Portes & Landolt, 1996) and if it is to bring benefit to society as a whole, it must be accessible by all society's members and not appropriated by sectional interests.

THE POLICY CLIMATE AND FAITH-BASED ORGANISATIONS

Faced with a plethora of approaches to giving meaning to such a slippery but politically useful term, policy-makers at the British Cabinet Office opted not for tight definition, but for a description of social capital as

> *all those institutional arrangements, networks and relationships which promote understanding, trust and mutual respect; allow communities to pursue shared goals more effectively; improve information flows; and generally improve the quality of life* (Cabinet Office, 1999, p. 137).

It is not hard to see how such a loose and inclusive description of social capital has contributed to a policy climate that provides a new context for the operation of voluntary and community bodies in the UK. The voluntary sector has been 'mainstreamed' into public policy through mechanisms like the Compact and the Active Community Unit (Kendall, 2000). Churches and other faith-based organisations have become a focus of government interest as the significance of the local initiatives in which they are often engaged has become clearer. Policymakers in Britain have not been slow to recognise a potential synergy between the aims and practices of faith groups and policy objectives relating to neighbourhood renewal and social inclusion. A growing body of academic evidence of the impact of the work of religious congregations upon social disadvantage became available in the 1990s (Cameron, 1996, 1998; Harris, 1994, 1995, 1998). More recently it has come increasingly from churches themselves (Drummond et al., 2002; Finneron et al., 2001; Rossiter, 2002). *Faith in the City* (ACUPA, 1985), in rallying the churches and challenging government, was a landmark document. It gave life to the work of the Church Urban Fund that ensued (Farnell et al., 1994) and led to experiments in the application to British cities of American approaches to community organising through the churches (Furbey et al., 1997). A major statement from the Catholic Bishops of England and Wales was also published in the 1990s. Out of the social teaching of the Catholic Church it provided a theological framework for the promotion of 'community and the common good' (Catholic Bishops Conference of England and Wales, 1996).

In the United States church congregations have been promoted as the solution to the perceived crisis in American welfare (Cnaan & Boddie, 2002; Cnaan, Wineburg & Boddie, 1999; Sherman, 2000; Wineburg, 1998). The controversial 'Charitable Choice' clause in the Personal Responsibility and Work Opportunity Reconciliation Act 1996 was designed to overturn the established practice of denying government funding to 'pervasively sectarian' organisations like church congregations (Center for Public Justice, 1996). The Bush Administration created an Office for Faith-Based and Community Initiatives within the White House with the task of returning the operation of government funded community services to local community groups, especially congregations and faith-based organisations. The White House Report *Unlevel Playing Field* presented initial findings on barriers impeding religious organisations seeking to serve the common good in collaboration with Federal Government. It came in response to an executive order issued by the President in which he said

> *The paramount goal is compassionate results, and private and charitable groups, including religious ones, should have the fullest*

opportunity permitted by law to compete on a level playing field, so long as they achieve valid public purposes .... (Bush, 2001).

The UK is some way from American policy on faith-based organisations and the accompanying controversy. But growing Westminster awareness of their potential is seen in Tony Blair's Tawney Lecture in March 2001 underlining the scope for partnership between government and churches in work to tackle social exclusion (Blair, 2001a). It runs through the training materials produced by the Department of the Environment, Transport and the Regions to enable faith-based organisations to become more effective in community development and urban regeneration work (Chester et al., 1999). It surfaces in reports of the Policy Action Teams set up by the cross-departmental Social Exclusion Unit to investigate possibilities for neighbourhood renewal (Home Office, 1999). In the PAT 17 report it recommends that Local Strategic Partnerships include faith communities (Home Office, 2000). The New Deal for Communities programme represents a partnership between government and faith communities in regeneration initiatives and ways to tackle deprivation (Wells, 2001a). It is demonstrated by the Prime Minister's appointment of an unofficial personal representative with faith groups 'to listen thoughtfully and take soundings' (Church Times, 21/12/01). It is the force that has driven the Local Government Association to produce its publication *Faith and Community*. This good practice guide explicitly encourages local authorities to develop partnerships with faith communities and to recognise that churches and other faith groups are an important and distinct part of the voluntary sector (LGA, 2002).

Northern Ireland has also seen significant changes to the context within which the voluntary and community sector operates. As in Wales (Chaney & Fevre, 2001), these changes are not only in the institutional and funding environment, but also in the constitutional arrangements (Kearney & Williamson, 2001). The NI Executive's first Programme for Government, Spring 2001, set out a key role for the sector and recognised the importance of involving it in policies and programmes aimed at strengthening community wellbeing. It also committed the Executive to encourage and support greater community participation, especially from those groups under-represented in voluntary activities and to increase the number of active community groups and volunteers. However, unlike the thrust of central policy initiatives based in London, the programme did not go out of its way to embrace faith communities.

The reasons for this reluctance may relate to the problematic nature of religion and politics in Northern Ireland to which allusion has already been made. Or they may have to do with the fact that the definition of the voluntary sector followed by the NI Community and Voluntary Sector Almanac virtually excludes churches, asserting that they exist 'solely for the benefit of their members' (NICVA, 2002, p.13). A Belfast conference in April 2002 provided the context for a revealing moment when the Secretary of the Department for Social Development, acknowledging that 'churches have much more to offer people beyond the traditional rites of birth, marriage and death', went on to speak of his Department as 'keen to work in partnership with the *community sector*' (italics added). He stopped short of specifying partnership with churches as such. There was no word from the Department about central government policy objectives to build the capacity of faith-based organisations, to facilitate and promote neighbourhood partnerships that include faith communities and to reduce barriers to such communities accessing public funding for community initiatives. This was despite the fact that he was speaking in the premises of a church-based organisation to an audience of church-based community workers (Salt and Pepper, 2002).

WHY THIS PROJECT?

Given such apparent sensitivities about the voluntary sector, the complexities surrounding faith-based organisations and the ambiguities of social capital as a concept, it might be asked why a project should link the three within the additional particularities of the Northern Ireland context.

First, it is timely to draw the attention of both churches and policy-makers to the body of empirical evidence about the public benefit work of churches that is now available from the international third sector research effort of the last ten years. Odd as it may seem, churches in Northern Ireland may not themselves be aware of the significance of this evidence. Churches were responding to human need long before the current government interest in enhancing their work or harnessing it to public policy concerns. They are likely to continue whether or not their work fits the instrumental designs of government policy. It is just what they do as churches. It is not something that they proclaim as self-conscious actors within the voluntary sector. For this very reason they can all too easily and, in the view of this report, mistakenly be defined out of the voluntary sector and their public benefit work be overlooked.

Research has established that religion is a major motivating factor for voluntary action in organised form (Greeley, 1997; James, 1987). Religions are traditionally rooted in communities and have an interest in and record of promoting positive community values (Sarkis, 2001). Through their organisations they can deliver community services and provide education. Evidence has emerged of links between the practice of a faith and health, employment and citizenship. The literature shows faith communities, with their congregations and other organisations, as diverse in purpose and manner of organising (Jeavons, 1998). Their members are likely to be active in non-religious parts of civil society (James, 1987). They may well provide the financial and human capital to start other voluntary enterprises (Chaves, 1998). Through the beliefs they sustain, they mandate philanthropy and justice-seeking activities by their members (Wuthnow, 1991). They are often quick to respond to the needs of disadvantaged people (Cameron, 1998; Cnaan, 1999; Harris, 1995; Wineburg, 1994). Their witness to real human need may trigger the creation of welfare programmes (Cnaan et al., 2002). All this is evidence of what churches can do and of what some are actually doing elsewhere. The question is, are churches engaged in any similar activities in Northern Ireland? This report argues that, if they are, then they can neither be defined out of the voluntary sector on the basis that 'their activities are solely for the benefit of their members' (NICVA, 2002 p.13) nor excluded from the public policy framework.

Second, it is worth framing church-related voluntary action in social capital terms because, as the emerging work of Community Evaluation Northern Ireland shows (Morrissey & McGinn, 2001), these are the terms in which voluntary action is currently understood and evaluated by policy-makers. Elsewhere in the UK the profile of the social capital represented by faith communities is significant enough for government to incorporate them within the strategy for neighbourhood renewal. If, as is promised on the second page of the Social Exclusion Unit report, *A New Commitment to Neighbourhood Renewal* (Cabinet Office, 2001), this national strategy is drawn upon by the Northern Ireland and other regional administrations, and if a similar policy encouraging faith groups to participate in local regeneration is extended to Northern Ireland as departmental support for the Churches Community Work Alliance suggests it may be (DSD, 2002), then there is no time to lose in building information about the scope and nature of church-related voluntary action across the province.

Finally the research approach adopted for this project uses a social capital lens because of the affinity of social capital with religion. At first sight there might appear to be little or no connection. Yet, as is discussed in section 7 of this report, religion is about the elements that are central to social capital, namely relationships, interactions and trust. Ideas that have been developed around social capital can help in understanding the importance to wider society of some of the theological thinking that underpins the life and work of churches. Ideas that have long been familiar to members of faith communities can acquire contemporary leverage when interpreted and presented within a social capital framework. It is worth noting that one prominent shaper of the social capital debate, a member of the World Bank Development Research Group and Harvard lecturer in public policy, has turned his thoughts in this direction. In a paper dated July 2002 he identifies complementary ideas from the realms of development practice, social science and theology and finds what he calls 'encouraging synergies'. He writes that

> *the theology, theory, and strategy of development cooperation are all about 'getting the social relations right'. Persistent poverty is both a symptom and a cause of a world in which the social relations are in some fundamental sense 'wrong'. Living the life that God intends for us all - one in which we more perfectly reflect his glory - will entail a concerted effort by rich, poor, and mediators alike to get them 'right'. It is the particular burden of faith communities to take up this challenge...* (Woolcock, 2002).

It is not necessary to share Michael Woolcock's view here to be struck by the novelty of such a suggestion by a social scientist.

The overall aim of the project here reported on could be expressed in terms of an exploration of how far churches and other faith-based organisations have been willing to take up the challenge that Woolcock identifies. The research set out to shed light on the nature, range and effectiveness of any public benefit contribution currently being made by churches and other FBOs in Northern Ireland. It sought to learn more about the social capital that might exist in such bodies, whether it represents a reservoir of resources that can be mobilised to strengthen social wellbeing, to build social cohesion and combat social exclusion. It looked for, and found, signs that faith-based organisations can be social bridges between segregated sectarian communities.

SECTION 2   PROJECT DESIGN AND IMPLEMENTATION

The section lays out the aims of the project and provides information about the initial research design and methodology employed for meeting them.

AIMS AND OBJECTIVES

As set out in the terms of reference, two broad aims are at the heart of this project.

The first is:
> 'to identify examples of church-related voluntary action which offer potential for the social capital formation necessary to promote church and community coordination of social resources in addressing community issues'.

The second is:
> 'to produce data and analyses which will increase understanding of the relationships between churches and their respective communities in Northern Ireland'.

These aims are broken down into four objectives.

- To add to existing knowledge and understanding of the role of the churches in their respective communities in Northern Ireland; in particular with regard to their work in providing welfare services and facilities and, specifically, in generating bridging social capital.

- To provide empirical data which identifies, measures and differentiates the exercise of that role in different communities.

- To identify trends, assess quality and enhance knowledge and understanding of community-related church activities that are demonstrably beneficial.

- To explore the relevance of concepts such as 'leadership', 'sustaining community cohesion', 'cross-community benefit' in the context of the church/community relationship.

Section 2 Project Design and Implementation 31

RESEARCH DESIGN

In a research approach combining elements of qualitative and quantitative methods, the project was designed to fall into three phases.

Phase 1. Survey and telephone interviews. Targets were:

- To select 12 churches or other faith-based organisations (FBOs) for study;
- To arrange research access;
- To despatch survey questionnaires A and B to 1 identified leader of each FBO and to 2 additional respondents identified by the leadership (Questionnaire A to focus on voluntary service activity, B on social capital);
- To conduct 36 semi-structured telephone interviews, 3 respondents from each of the 12 FBOs;
- To compile an analysis and an interim report.

Phase 2. Case studies. Targets were:

- To select 5 FBOs for case study on the basis of data from Phase 1;
- To conduct 25 in-depth face-to-face semi-structured interviews (5 interviews per organisation) to explore the themes emerging in Phase 1;
- To analyse data.

Phase 3. Write up and dissemination. Targets were:

- To prepare the final report;
- To arrange a dissemination event;
- To draft academic articles.

Phase 1 comprised a trawl for churches and other faith-based organisations (FBOs) suitable for examination and the selection of twelve from across Northern Ireland, taking in both Belfast and a spread of provincial towns. Information was to be generated by means of a postal survey delivered to 36 respondents and through 36 semi-structured telephone interviews with the leadership of the selected twelve organisations. The interviews were to be guided by a schedule sent in advance to respondents.

Phase 2 covered the choice of five of the twelve FBOs for case study through 25 face-to-face semi-structured interviews.

Phase 3 referred to the analysis of all data, preparation of the project report and its dissemination. Throughout the duration of the project the global discourse on social capital was to be monitored.

The following changes were made to the initial design. The rationale for these is offered in Appendix II.

- The two Phase 1 survey questionnaires (A and B) were combined into one. Ten of these were distributed to each FBO, making a total of 120 instead of the 72 originally intended.

- A total of 46 face-to-face interviews was conducted (3 each for 7 profiles; 5 each for 5 case studies) instead of 36 by telephone and 25 face-to-face as in the original design.

SAMPLING ISSUES

Profiles

Sampling was of necessity purposive. It does not pretend to be representative. The original proposal limited the project to an examination of twelve organisations. A figure greater than twelve was seen as unrealistic for a single researcher in the time available. Fewer than twelve would not cover the most common types of organisation to be found. The twelve had to include congregations and at least one example of a para-church organisation. They needed to reflect both the Belfast context and that of the provincial towns. Whether they told a story of success, failure, or both, they had to come from the widest possible range.

Section 2 Project Design and Implementation 33

No sampling frame comprehensive enough to cover the spectrum of organisations of interest to the study was available. Orientation began with deskwork. Church guides and directories were consulted as well as websites where they existed. Other documents produced by such bodies as the Irish Inter Church Meeting, Community Relations Council, Belfast Churches Urban Development Committee were helpful.

A rolling process identified some key informants. These included people from the churches, from the voluntary and community sector, from local government and from academia, all of whom could offer insights from their extensive working overview of church and community life in Northern Ireland. Soundings with these informants laid the foundation for working relationships and generated basic knowledge of the field. From these exchanges there emerged a list of possible organisations in an appropriate spread of locations with programmes that promised to provide examples of the kind of voluntary activity that the research aimed to find and investigate. This was action to bridge fracture lines in society, action that might be understood in terms of cross cutting, or 'bridging' social capital formation.

The project limited its exploration to Christian faith-based organisations for two reasons. First, although minority faith communities are growing in the population of Northern Ireland, figures from the NI Inter-Faith Forum show that they remain relatively small in numbers. Second, minority faith communities are not implicated in the historic divisions within Northern Ireland.

The most obvious and widespread of Christian faith-based organisations are the congregations of the churches. Of these, the four 'main' denominations make up 80 percent (unadjusted) of the population (NI Census, 2001 Religion Report). Since they represent distinct groupings with more than religious differences, it was clearly essential to address them all. Thus Roman Catholic, Presbyterian, Church of Ireland and Methodist congregations were included in the study. Given the numerical weakening of the traditional churches and the formation of 'new' churches in Northern Ireland as in the rest of the UK, it was decided to include an example of the small, but growing, LifeLink Network of Churches.

Beyond congregations, the world of para-churches and other organisations emerging from a faith base presents a variety of organisational type, purpose, scale and affiliation that would require a research project in its own right. The task was therefore to ensure that, when taken together, the selected FBOs included both congregations and para-churches encompassing a full range of exemplars from the main denominations, constitutional arrangements and activities, in order to provide a richness of data.

As to geographical location Belfast, with its large population, presented the greatest variety of organisation and scope for choice. Over half of the sample came from that city. On the question of which provincial towns to include in the study, a telephone trawl, followed in some cases by local investigative visits, provided a means of identifying possible FBOs.

Ultimately a single crucial factor influenced the choice of FBOs for the study. Each one had to show some kind of evidence of engagement with the local community. Irrespective of the location, buildings and financial arrangements, the number and type of staff, the membership strength and characteristics of each chosen FBO, its activity had to hold the promise of demonstrating some benefit beyond its own membership.

Case studies

The selection of organisations for case study was left until after consideration of the material generated in the Phase 1 interviews and the relationships that were in place by then. Where the profiles were of necessity somewhat formulaic and factual, the case studies were intended to provide a richer texture so that, taken together, they would be suggestive of a process of formation of social capital.

Five possibilities emerged which met the need to balance affiliation, location and type of organisation. Affiliation included Roman Catholic, Presbyterian, Church of Ireland and New Church congregations, with an additional one that was unaffiliated to any denominational grouping. Three of the cases were Belfast based and two were in provincial towns. Two para-churches and three congregations with para-type offshoots were chosen. The eventual group of five was manageable in terms of scope of operation and distance from the researcher's base at Coleraine.

NEGOTIATING ACCESS

The process of negotiating access and of gaining the cooperation of the leaders proved to be delicate and time consuming. Where these organisations were churches the approach was possible either through individual local leaders or through the headquarter bodies. Experience suggested the local approach in the first instance and this was broadly effective, in that preliminary interviews soon dissolved any initial reservations about the degree to which sensitive issues would be probed. In the case of one religious denomination, however, informal approaches were unsatisfactory and it took formal representation at senior level to open the door to secure the goodwill and assistance necessary for this study.

A letter was drafted and an explanation of the purposes of the project prepared for the leader of each FBO. Before mailing this background material an exploratory telephone call was the first step in the process of negotiating access. In the course of these conversations it became clear that the proposed semi-structured telephone interviews would be more satisfactorily conducted face-to-face (See Appendix II).

INTERVIEW SCHEDULE AND SURVEY QUESTIONNAIRE

The interview schedule is included as Appendix III. The survey questionnaires A and B were combined into one during the process of drafting them for piloting in Phase 1. The rationale for this is explained in Appendix II. Each organisation received 10 questionnaires, making for an optimal return of 120. (The response was in fact 88). This did not alleviate the difficulties facing any attempt to get an empirical grip on social capital. Appendix I provides some insight into the complexities of designing a questionnaire that will tie down such an elusive concept. Assistance was drawn from the work of Onyx and Bullen (1997), the World Values Survey and from instruments already developed for surveying religious attitudes in Northern Ireland (Boal et al., 1997). Research proceeded on the basis that the project was a qualitative study first, albeit one that would be supported by relevant quantitative data extracted from the questionnaire returns.

SECTION 3 *PROFILES OF TWELVE FAITH-BASED ORGANISATIONS*

The section presents profiles of the twelve organisations, built up from the interviews, under the following headings: Type, Objectives, Activities, Buildings, Participation, Resourcing and use of research, Linkages and Cross-community dimension.

The immediate setting of each of the organisations now addressed has its unique local combination of characteristics. Common to all is an overall context of industrial decline and persisting economic difficulty. Though clusters of prosperity exist, unemployment remains high and associated hardship has affected the foundations of both extended and nuclear family life. The built environment is stressed and housing redevelopment has fragmented many traditional communities. The daunting social climate has been exacerbated by the years of conflict. In some areas paramilitaries have a strong grip and there are problems with alcohol abuse, drug related and other crime. This makes for an uncomfortable context within which to work across community boundaries. When it is remembered that Northern Ireland is a geographically small place, the reader will understand why names of people and places have been changed where requested.

Table 2. FBO by name, type, denominational background and location

	FBO Name	FBO Type	FBO Denomination	FBO Location
1	Flax	Para-church	Catholic based	Belfast
2	Holy Family	Parish	Catholic	Belfast
3	Boys and Girls Club	Para-church	Catholic based	Omagh
4	Ballysillan	Congregation	Presbyterian	Belfast
5	'Benmoe'	Congregation	Presbyterian	'Ballycarn'
6	Knocknagoney	Parish	Church of Ireland	Belfast
7	Shankill	Parish	Church of Ireland	Lurgan
8	City Mission	Congregation	Methodist	Londonderry
9	Barnabas	Para-church	Methodist based	Enniskillen
10	YMCA (Central)	Para-church	Cross denominational	Belfast
11	Oasis	Para-church	New Church based	Belfast
12	Mornington	Para-church	Unaffiliated	Belfast

The previous table shows the 12 faith-based organisations in the study by name, by type, by denominational background and by location. It will be noted that 6 are para-churches and 6 are churches, designated as either congregation or parish. Of

Section 3 Profiles of Twelve Faith-based Organisations   37

the 12 FBOs, 3 are identified with a Catholic base, 2 Presbyterian, 2 Church of Ireland, 2 Methodist, 1 cross denominational, 1 New Church and 1 unaffiliated.

PROFILE 1: A CATHOLIC BASED CHARITABLE TRUST, FLAX BELFAST

Type

Flax is a charitable trust with a twelve-strong board that was established in a Catholic parish in the late 1970s. It is located in Ardoyne, a predominantly Catholic area in the north of Belfast that has seen several hundred sectarian murders in some of the most intense civil unrest in Northern Ireland.

Objectives

The mission statement of Flax Trust states that it exists for the relief of poverty, dependency and chronic unemployment and under-employment in Northern Ireland as well as the reduction and elimination of community tensions and religious prejudices engendered by the economic depression of the area. With reconciliation as its long term goal, this organisation seeks opportunity to bring together people with different viewpoints, Catholic and Protestant, community and professional, lay and religious, to develop and implement an appropriate strategy for the social and economic regeneration through which that goal may be achieved.

Activities

The trust oversees a range of autonomous business and community organisations. On the business side, on-site live-in accommodation is part of the package for deprived young people undergoing training towards IT industry standards that the organisation's business school offers. Programmes provide training that leads to guaranteed jobs. An employment facilitation project allows long-term unemployed people (up to 59 years of age) to enter a work preparation scheme. Open Learning resources encourage adults back to education. Two in-house internet servicing companies provide training, consulting and banking facilities otherwise unavailable to those with lower budgets. On the community and cultural side of the operation, craft units and an arts centre comprising theatre, dance studio and gallery are used as vehicles for inter-community reconciliation. A drop-in centre offers programmes for adolescents and young adults perceived as being outside the main line in youth provision or 'not wanted by other clubs' in the area. A cross-community group oversees services to disabled people, single parents and senior citizens, including preparation and delivery of meals on wheels. A community magazine is produced monthly.

Flax also runs a shopping complex which includes a health centre incorporating a GP and practice nurse service; a dental surgery; a women's programme; bereavement support; services for elderly people, respite for carers, and varied social activities. There is also a housing association. The community association with a group of locally elected street representatives, dating from the beginnings of Flax, constitutes an important arm of its work. Through a community house it provides advice on welfare benefits and housing and other problems. A home safety and energy scheme for elderly people and low-income families, a cross-community environmental landscaping project, a housing improvement programme and local traffic calming measures are in place. The association has cross-community and cross-border contacts. Its women's forum has produced a book entitled *Living with Poverty*, written by women from Catholic and Protestant backgrounds.

Buildings

These activities, along with the administrative headquarters, are based in a former linen mill with an estimated workspace of a quarter of a million square feet. Situated at a flashpoint on one of the interfaces between Catholic and Protestant communities in north Belfast, the mill was purchased in 1977 and converted into units for the incubation of small businesses. It also houses the arts centre and accommodation units for youth trainees. The shopping complex and health centre are nearby, as are some of the houses built in cooperation with the Salvation Army. The trust's local community association operates a community house.

Participation

On a daily basis over 1500 people are said to engage in the commercial, social, educational or cultural activities of this FBO, whether as employees, volunteers or clients. This is an estimate by the founding director. Other estimations are indicative of the reach of this organisation: of the three hundred and twenty businesses incubated since its beginnings 60 percent were set up by Protestant people; of the five thousand people placed in employment through the trust's training programmes in that same time 50 percent were Catholic. Despite its size, larger than any other FBO in this study, it remains anchored in the local setting. Community participation and cooperation are encouraged through a locally representative association. The community magazine, a 32 page local production, is said to reach some 10,000 readers at home and overseas each month. Projects are developed in response to suggestions by the community association and in consultation with professional, government and trust representation. Local people are included among board members. Local pride in the centre and ownership of its activities are reported to be high.

Resourcing and use of research

There is a high level of professionalism, sophistication in public relations and financial backing secured. Flax has offices in Belfast, Dublin and New York and draws on the support of 63 funders from government departments, through British, Irish and American foundations to international religious organisations and other bodies. From small early beginnings the trust has grown to become a significant player in the economics of the city of Belfast and beyond. Research has played an important part in this growth. One example of the trust's careful use of research is its work identifying need by using deprivation indicators. This enabled it to build the case for a new type of health centre.

Linkages

The trust has co-operative links with bodies of many different kinds. There are partnerships with statutory bodies: with a health and social services trust in relation to the health centre; with the Northern Ireland Housing Executive in connection with a housing improvement programme promoted by the community association. Partnerships have been formed with various large private sector organisations and firms to tailor programmes that guarantee jobs in, for example, engineering and construction for those in the trust's training schemes. A partnership has been built with another FBO, the Salvation Army (SA) in order to make available supported housing units for elderly people and emergency and short-term accommodation for homeless families and single women until they are resettled through the SA's rehabilitation and training programme. Over one hundred further new housing units are in the pipeline.

Cross-community dimension

Inevitably the trust reflects its majority Catholic context and beginnings. However it expresses a cross-community dimension wherever possible, from the religiously mixed body of people on its board to its joint work with the Salvation Army, from its facilitation of Protestant business entrepreneurs to its preparation and delivery of meals to all and any in the neighbourhood who need them.

PROFILE 2: A CATHOLIC PARISH, HOLY FAMILY BELFAST

Type

Holy Family Catholic parish dates back to the final decade of the nineteenth century. Located in north Belfast, it covers an extensive area from the edge of the inner city to the fringe of the city boundary, from rows of old terrace housing to new upmarket starter homes, including on the way established villas once the residences of well to do merchant and shipping families. In places it touches on adjacent Protestant Loyalist territory and there are flashpoints along the line. Within the boundary the population is roughly 80 percent Catholic. At the lower end it is uniformly Catholic working/non-working class.

Objectives

The main objective, expressed in the mission statement is 'to create a praying, caring community, centred in Christ'. There is a conscious effort to teach people to understand that they are 'loved by God' and that 'they have a responsibility to one another'. Three church buildings in the parish offer daily opportunity for prayer. Care and community building activities touch those both in and beyond the membership of the parish.

Activities

Support groups and other societies that are traditional in such a parish encourage the practice of caring. St Vincent de Paul offers assistance to anyone in need. The Pioneer Association promotes responsible attitudes to alcohol. A credit union is long established. There are groups for young men, for physically disabled people and for those with learning difficulties, uniformed groups for young folk, awareness-raising groups of one kind or another. The parish runs a house for homeless families. A youth resource centre provides a structured programme for the personal and social development of young people in the 5-25 age range, with the members themselves involved in the planning, organising and management of the activities. Older people from all sections of the community find opportunity to make new friends, pursue personal interests and develop new skills at the day centre, at which a carer support service is also based. A parish centre provides an outlet for recreational activities and a pastoral centre offers educational courses promoting spiritual, personal and academic growth.

A sense of belonging is actively fostered. Every home within the boundary of the parish received an invitation for people to sign a document declaring that they were members. People who thus actively identify with the parish receive a directory providing details of worship, information about people and groups, services and activities, welcoming all and carrying the message that no one is excluded from these things. The opportunity to express views about aspects of parish life is provided through surveys of all registered parishioners over sixteen years of age.

People are made aware of the needs, opportunities and costs facing the parish and invited to make a contribution. Through pre-school provision, the parish schools try to build a strong partnership between parents, teachers, children and the community in order to maximise each child's development. They have a major influence within the parish by the ways in which they strengthen identity, engender a sense of social responsibility and increase awareness of wider issues like third world needs and the global environment.

Buildings

There are three church buildings and six Catholic schools, a nursery, two primary and three secondary-level school complexes in the parish. A youth club occupies its own dedicated base in a building that is part of one of the church complexes. Other premises include a day centre for elderly people, a parish hall and a pastoral centre. Housing is provided for the clergy.

Participation

Upwards of 7,800 individual people are registered with the parish office. The parish team has 6 members made up of four priests, a parish sister and an office manager. A pastoral council of 10 voluntary members works closely with the team to identify and tackle the spiritual, social and community needs of the parish, setting up task groups to give attention to local issues like bereavement, suicide, and drug and alcohol abuse. The wider paid staff group includes a secretary, three sacristans, four housekeepers, two caretakers and a maintenance worker. Schoolteachers are paid by the Department of Education, as are the two youth club leaders.

There is a pool of some 900 volunteers. The voluntary activity based in and/or supported by the church is highlighted by exhibitions held in the parish. These serve to celebrate, exchange information, heighten awareness and aid recruitment. Just as the pastoral council gives local people a voice in planning and decision-making, parish ministries offer them roles at liturgical services in the three churches.

Resourcing and use of research

Apart from the schools, funding is mostly internal and voluntary with some statutory support. There has been little formal research on the characteristics of the parish area. A census carried out to update parish records was followed by a survey of attitudes to faith and religious practice in the parish. A high proportion of the population identifies with Holy Family. Knowledge of the nature and needs of the local area is immediately available through the large membership.

Linkages

Organisational links exist with Health and Social Services, the Department of Education, Belfast City Council, the local Partnership Board and two community development groups. There are cooperative links with local businesses and banks and with other churches in the area. International Catholic charities are well supported and a link with a parish in Fiji involves schoolchildren and others in friendships and exchange visits.

Cross-community dimension

Cross-community activity has a focus in the day centre which is run on interdenominational lines. The founders of a cross-community support group for widows and victims of the conflict are members of this church. The schools offer cross-community contact in addition to the curriculum and their range of extra-curricular activities. The youth club has similar links across the community divide. St Vincent de Paul, here as elsewhere, works across the community with people in need irrespective of denomination. It provides and runs a short-term accommodation facility for up to eleven families that is open to anyone of any background referred by statutory services.

A faith development course (Alpha) is presented and welcomes people from across the whole community with the support of leaders of the local Protestant churches. An inter-church group organises ecumenical events and promotes respect for religious differences. Clergy meet regularly with colleagues from the other churches of the area and there is occasional shared worship. One small group has moved into the sensitive field of social and political cross-community work and has relinquished its formal links with the parish though many of the same people remain involved.

Further information appears in case study 3 page 80.

PROFILE 3: A CATHOLIC BASED COMPANY, BOYS AND GIRLS CLUB OMAGH

Type

Omagh Boys and Girls Club is a charitable organisation with a management committee overseen by nine trustees who form Omagh Youth and Community Trust, a company limited by guarantee. It has been in existence since 1952 when it was formed by the priest and the young people of the Catholic parish of Drumragh.

Objectives

The main purpose of the club is to facilitate activity-based youth work through a sporting, social and educational programme which is planned by a group that includes the young people themselves and for which they take some responsibility through positions on the management committee.

Activities

Members participate in a range of sports and may represent the club at football, netball, badminton, basketball and boxing fixtures at home or away. Creative arts based work offers opportunities for music, dance and drama. Computer training is provided. There are specific projects for young women and for young men treating issues of relationships, skills development and confidence building. A playgroup and after school group are boosted throughout July by a daily summer scheme.

Buildings

The club occupied a series of premises on the southern side of the town since its beginnings. In 2001 it moved into a purpose-built centre on the site of an old station yard by the town railway station on the former Belfast to Derry line. The new home of the club allows expansion and further development of activities. The complex includes a sports hall and fully equipped changing rooms, a dedicated playgroup area, a rehearsal and performance level for arts work, a computer suite, an extensive social area with facilities for light refreshments, smaller rooms for project and committee work and administrative offices. There is a club minibus.

Participation

The new centre is in use for at least six out of every seven days and sees about 1500 young people using its facilities each week. There are 15 male and 5 female staff of whom 9 are volunteers. The staff team is headed by a full-time leader and a full-time youth tutor. The level of local ownership is high, with a strong loyalty to the Catholic origins and parish based tradition of the club. In an attempt to develop a more inclusive atmosphere it is now a policy requirement that all activities and programmes demonstrate a contribution to cross-community contact.

Resourcing and use of research

The local Catholic parish donated the site on which the new centre stands. Support for the building of the premises came from the Department of the Environment; the Sports Council Northern Ireland Lottery Fund; the Department of Education for Northern Ireland; the European Regional Development Fund through the EU Special Support Programme for Peace and Reconciliation; the Community Fund (Lottery); Western Education and Library Board (Youth Service); the Department of Foreign Affairs Ireland (Anglo-Irish Division); National Youth Orchestra of

Section 3 Profiles of Twelve Faith-based Organisations   45

Ireland and SHARE, Cork; Boys and Girls Clubs of Northern Ireland; Lloyds TSB Foundation for Northern Ireland; the Rank Foundation. The effort to raise capital for the new building, the first purpose-built home for the club, and financial support for programmes began from scratch. There is now some expertise in accessing grants. The process necessitated research into local conditions and an economic appraisal was carried out, paid for by the Department of the Environment.

Linkages

Strong links with local churches are in place. There are informal links with Omagh District Council arts section and youth and community workers, with the Women's Area Network and with the Forum for Omagh Community Development. Professional links exist with Western Education and Library Board Youth Service, Northern Ireland Council for Voluntary Action, Irish Amateur Boxing Association and the Boys and Girls Clubs of Northern Ireland.

Cross-community dimension

In keeping with the policy of this organisation, a cross-community element is discernible in much of its activity, sometimes more, sometimes less intentional. The young women's group meets with a similar group from a Protestant youth club for a twelve week exploration of the meaning of identity. This incorporates cross-border liaison with a third group in the Republic of Ireland. The focus of the after schools group is on homework, but it brings together children from the county school as well as Catholic schools and the parents come to the club to collect them. The summer scheme brings together 50 volunteers and 200 children every day in July in a cross-community mix. The football teams from this club and from a neighbouring Protestant youth club travel away to play in tournaments together and have been doing so for some years. The Board of Trustees is made up of 5 Catholic and 4 Protestant people.

PROFILE 4: A PRESBYTERIAN CONGREGATION, BALLYSILLAN, BELFAST

Type

Ballysillan Presbyterian is a mainstream Protestant congregation with its own operational independence, established in the early nineteenth century in north

Belfast. In terms of religious territoriality, the locality represents a Protestant enclave within a wider area that is predominantly Catholic. This part of Belfast has been deeply affected by the social and political turbulence of the last thirty years and significant outward population movement has resulted in diminished Protestant numbers, with a bias toward older residents.

Objectives

The church has adopted no mission statement as such. The minister gave a flexible expression of the church's purpose as 'to be a happy, biblically faithful, God-honouring church'. As a congregation, the main objective is firstly to provide for worship and then for other needs, spiritual and temporal, of its members. However its work is not confined to the church membership, particularly its work with young people. It also acknowledges a responsibility to make a useful contribution to the local community, as was seen in minister's public mediation work throughout the Holy Cross dispute of autumn 2001.

Activities

In addition to services of worship, the range of activities engaged in by the people includes traditional uniformed organisations for boys and for girls, religious classes for young people, a fellowship group for teenage church people and a youth club that is open to non church members. There are women's meetings, a religious study group for 'ladies', a group for widows and widowers, an afternoon fellowship group for older members and an evening one that is not age-specific.

Buildings

As well as the church building itself, the organisation occupies two halls and suite of rooms in a compact complex that includes a new purpose-built lounge for youth work that was described as 'relationally-based'. A house is provided for the minister and his family.

Participation

Out of a membership of around 500 families some 85 volunteers contribute their time and energy to the church and community programmes and to the pastoral care of members of the congregation. Within the uniformed organisations for young people (Boys' Brigade and Girl Guides), led by 21 adult volunteers, over 70 percent of the 107 members have no other connection with the church. The non-uniformed organisations include Youth Club, Youth Fellowship, Bible Class and Sunday School. They are led by 18 adult volunteers. Some 75 percent of the 169 members have no other connection with the church. The 28 members of the Presbyterian Women's Association are served by 4 voluntary leaders. The 24 members of the Ladies' Bible Study Group are looked after by 1 voluntary leader and the 25 Senior Citizens by 4 volunteers. The prayer group and choir have 25 and 20 members respectively. A worker is employed to stabilise the congregation's 20 to 45 age group, to build bridges to the families of the youth club members and to represent the congregation in the local community. In addition, 37 members of this church serve the local community through various charitable or voluntary groups as school governors or participants in the local community forum. The minister reported a low level of local ownership of these activities.

Resourcing and use of research

In the mid 1990s the congregation invested significant energy and finance in the upgrading of youth facilities with substantial matching funding from government through Making Belfast Work (MBW). Smaller grants have been obtained for uniformed organisations and work with elderly people. Central church authorities contribute to the salary of the worker amongst the 20 - 45 age group. The Northern Ireland Housing Executive provides a house for community work and staffing support comes in the form of a placement at the church by an international religious development agency. Research has played a part in identifying both the strengths and weaknesses of the organisation and local needs to which attention might be appropriately directed. MBW (Making Belfast Work, Department of the Environment) support for the renovation of the lounge for work with young people was conditional upon an economic appraisal being carried out. The minister himself, supported by his central church authorities, undertook practice-based research that in turn informed and refined the congregation's stance on some of the social problems of the area. The organisation also looked for lessons from American church models.

Linkages

While the minister and some congregational members are embedded in local networks there are no formal links at congregational level. Linkages are more usual either through the presbytery, a grouping of neighbouring Presbyterian congregations, or through the sub units within the congregation, say, the Senior Citizens' group.

Cross-community dimension

There are no formal cross-community links, nor are there any church structures to encourage them. Good personal relationships across the divide are extensive and a project, under the umbrella of the YMCA, brought a group from this congregation into close contact with a nearby Catholic equivalent.

PROFILE 5: A PRESBYTERIAN CONGREGATION, 'BENMOE', 'BALLYCARN'

Type

'Benmoe' Presbyterian church was established in the 1970s in 'Ballycarn', a market town with a population of around 60,000 people. It was set up to serve a newly built mixed housing area with a population of 60/40 Protestant/Catholic. Originally an extension of an existing congregation, it is now independent.

Objectives

The mission statement describes this church as existing 'to worship God, grow through discipleship, love each other through fellowship and reach out in mission'. The current emphasis is on re-engaging with people in a surrounding community that has seen dramatic change.

Activities

Members meet for worship and for religious classes on Sundays and for prayer and study in midweek meetings. There are leadership opportunities for singers, musicians and teachers. There are uniformed organisations for young people and a youth club that attracts many with no other connection to the church. Two groups are run specifically by and for women and one for men, each providing an educational and social programme. An afternoon group offers social contact for older people. A team of volunteers shares pastoral care. This church operates a pastoral care centre on one of the estates in a block of flats rented from the Housing Executive. Here people may drop in any morning from Monday to Friday. There is growing uptake, especially from people living in nearby singles accommodation. A small youth club operates on the basis of one leader to three

Section 3 Profiles of Twelve Faith-based Organisations 49

young people. A homework club, a group for single mothers and a faith development course (Alpha) are also running. A contact centre for estranged fathers is at the advanced planning stage.

Buildings

The congregation's base is a church and hall complex located between areas of public and private housing. The minister and his family occupy the manse, at a convenient distance from the church.

Participation

Over 300 families are members of the congregation. They provide about 150 volunteers for the work of the church. The church employs a part-time office secretary and the full-time community and youth worker. This worker operates from the pastoral centre and is supported at the drop-in centre by 20 volunteers. The uniformed organisations, Boys' Brigade and Girls' Brigade, each serve a membership of about 50. The youth fellowship, with a focus on faith development, has 20 members and the more recreational youth club upwards of 60. Both the groups for women and the men's fellowship have an average of 50 members. The senior citizen's gathering attracts 70 people. The great majority of those who participate in these activities are members of the congregation. Ownership and involvement by the wider local community remains at a low level.

Resourcing and use of research

The current policy of this church is not to seek any external funding, but to finance and control its own operation. There has been little formal research. However the committee with oversight of the pastoral care centre have charged the community worker with the task of learning about the needs of people in the area. Through meeting people on the doorstep and at the centre, the worker has built up local knowledge. She has communicated this to the church through regular reports and through presentations to the congregation at worship.

Linkages

Organisational links are extensive. Benmoe is an associate member of the local partnership. This involves all five churches in the area including a Catholic one and a church of Christian Brethren. There are links with residents' associations, the NI Housing Executive, the youth service, schools and a further education college, a women's aid hostel, police, statutory services and various charitable bodies. A local councillor chairs the partnership.

Cross-community dimension

Clergy and other leaders meet regularly. Churches now try to do some things together where they have previously made individual efforts. The community worker is developing strong working relationships right across the spectrum. A project with Habitat for Humanity, presently under discussion, may go forward on a cross-community basis.

Further information appears in case study 1, page 68.

PROFILE 6: A CHURCH OF IRELAND PARISH, KNOCKNAGONEY, BELFAST

Type

This parish came into being in the 1960s to serve several housing estates being erected at that time on Belfast's eastern city boundary.

Objectives

The minister described the main objective of this organisation in terms of 'making the church real to people outside it' and his work as helping the congregation to see themselves as part of the community and to acknowledge their need of the community.

Activities

There is weekly worship and a Sunday school. A choir and organist lead the music at worship. A group of women, spanning the generations, pursues a programme of social, recreational, educational and religious interests. There is a company of the uniformed Girls' Brigade, an informal group for boys up to eleven years of age and another for teenagers of the church. A midweek fellowship meets regularly and every so often evolves into a faith development course (Alpha) that welcomes all comers. A number of elderly people, once active in a bowling club, still meet for friendship.

Section 3 Profiles of Twelve Faith-based Organisations   51

Buildings

The congregation occupies a church and hall complex on the same site and the minister and his family live in the rectory provided by the parish.

Participation

Some 420 families claim a link with this church, but the congregation for worship each Sunday rarely exceeds 100 people, 60 percent of whom are about 60 years of age and over. About 40 people take active responsibility, undertaking roles in worship, in leadership of parish organisations and in pastoral support. The monthly Mothers' Union and young wives' group has a membership of about 20. The weekly Bible study group has approximately 10 people. This number grows when an Alpha course runs for twelve weeks. The Sunday school has less than 10 regular attenders and the choir about 15 singers. There are 16 Explorers (boys to 11) and 4 Pathfinders (teenage boys) meeting weekly. The Girls' Brigade, 60 strong, attracts the bulk of its members from those who do not attend Sunday worship. Engagement with the community is manifest in the joint management of the new church hall. A care group at an embryonic stage intends to collaborate with church people in visiting elderly residents in the area. The sense of local ownership is strengthening, according to the minister.

Resourcing and use of research

Support for the major refurbishment of the hall was procured from the Church of Ireland at central and diocesan level, from Belfast Regeneration Office, Belfast European Partnership Board, Urban Development Grant Department of the Department of the Environment and other funders. Formal research, including an economic appraisal of the locality, was carried out in preparation for application for funding for the renovation of church buildings. The diocese in which this parish is situated now requires a measure of strategic planning by its congregations.

Linkages

The minister has connections with a local school and is involved in management of a community association and other agencies in the neighbourhood. He meets regularly with his Presbyterian colleague and his wide personal links have led to co-operation with other people who have concerns about social need in the area.

It is intended that a team of visitors from the congregation will liaise with a local community care group. Informal links exist with Belfast City Council, East Belfast Community Development Association, NI Housing Executive, East Belfast Churches Forum and YMCA. The congregation is in a formal partnership with a local community association. A number of representatives of the church and of the community together oversee the running of the refurbished hall, now called the Aslan Centre.

Cross-community dimension

There is no proactive cross-community work at organisational level in this 'mostly loyalist' area. Personal contacts exist and two members of the congregation are known to be active in reconciliation work.

PROFILE 7: A CHURCH OF IRELAND PARISH, SHANKILL, LURGAN

Type

Shankill, one of the largest parishes of the Church of Ireland, was established early in the eighteenth century in Lurgan, a town of about 22,000 people divided evenly between Protestant and Catholic residents. Tensions have run high here and violence has erupted frequently during the period of the Troubles (1969 - 1994), and since.

Objectives

The vision statement declares this church to be 'a welcoming Christian community enabling more people to experience and express the reconciling love of God'.

Activities

This organisation provides a range of activities covered by nine departments of ministry. These are designated (alphabetically) Administrative and Support, Music, Outreach, Pastoral, Select Vestry, Seniors', World Mission and Audio Visual, Young Families' and Youth Ministries. Each department has a leader/coordinator. A facilitator serves this team of nine and the minister provides the focus of overall leadership.

The Administrative and Support Ministry includes services categorised as auxiliary staff, catering and hospitality, project minibuses, diocesan bridge building, parish magazine. Members also look after major refurbishment plans for some parish buildings, a breakfast and after school club, a programme for parents and children and several caring, support and welcome teams. The Music Ministry embraces a music group, organists and two choirs. Outreach Ministry involves work with a faith development course, bookstall, bellringing, family services, home groups, home mission, women's groups, recreational groups and a programme for encouraging potential volunteers.

Pastoral Ministries covers bereavement counselling, confirmation, harvest and Christmas gift distribution, contact with schools, hospitals and homes, lay visiting teams, marriage preparation, prayer ministries. The Select Vestry in the Church of Ireland is the committee elected to look after the fabric, furniture, and finance of the organisation. Members are also responsible for a support fund for missionaries from the parish and protection of children under Safeguarding Trust. The Seniors' Ministry co ordinates activities at the friendship centre, tape visitors and groups designated Cedars and Palms.

The World Mission department promotes five international missionary societies and one relief agency. Young Families involves work with baptism candidates and toddlers, social events and GLAMS - girls, ladies and mums of Shankill. Youth Ministries supports uniformed organisations (Boys' Brigade, Scouts and Guides) and a range of other groups, each with its own focus, (Crusaders, Kids' Kingdom, summer school and Easter club, Sunday schools, young adults' group, youth club and youth group).

The church formed an umbrella organisation in 1992, Shankill Parish Caring Association (SPCA), a company limited by guarantee with charitable status. SPCA qualifies for statutory assistance and can access funding for its initiatives in social action, community development and cross-community work. Examples of these initiatives are Shankill Seniors' Group, Shankill Youth Group, Kidz Patch, Lurgan Community Bridges Project, Jethro Centre proposals and PAKT Lurgan.

Buildings

As well as a house for the minister and his family, the buildings owned and operated by the parish include the large parish church, the nearby complex of parochial hall, minor hall, offices and lounge. Elsewhere in the parish the St Andrew's suite of facilities, to be redeveloped as the Jethro Centre, houses activities which are 4 percent church, the rest community use.

Participation

There are upwards of 1400 people who claim a link with the congregation. Of about 350 registered members, over 200 are active volunteers. Leadership of the activities sketched above requires 11 staff working full-time and 12 part-time along with a pool of volunteers. The magazine visitors' team, for example, is 120 strong, all of whom are volunteers. The Monday to Friday programmes for the Seniors' Group engage up to 400 people each week. About 350 young people are involved in Youth Group activities and 80 attend the Saturday night youth club. Some 140 families are involved in the PAKT project. These initiatives have obvious and significant local ownership and support. One of them, the PAKT concept, has been 'franchised' through the National Council of YMCAs in six locations in Ireland, north and south.

Resourcing and use of research

A considerable degree of sophistication has been developed in relation to accessing funding. Of the 23 staff mentioned above, the congregation funds 6 full-time and 6 part-time posts. Under the SPCA umbrella the remaining 5 full-time and 6 part-time workers are paid from other sources in a cocktail of external funding. An appropriate accompanying level of research has been employed to identify both the contours of local need and the landscape of funding opportunity. A business development group exists for the single purpose of exploring funding opportunities and developing proposals.

Linkages

Organisational links are extensive at home and abroad, within and beyond the church. As an officer of the diocese, the minister is integrated within wider denominational structures. The parish has connections with mission partners throughout the world. Some members have been on placements in Kazakhstan, Uruguay, Honduras and Japan. There is a strong relationship with a congregation

Section 3 Profiles of Twelve Faith-based Organisations   55

in the United States. Taking local examples from the SPCA initiatives, the Jethro Project proposal builds upon the success of programmes already in place. For this project, SPCA formed a partnership with Craigavon Borough Council on a £2 million proposal backed by statutory bodies within the area. Another shared enterprise links the Caring Association and the friends of a local primary school in Kidz Patch, a daily breakfast and after school club.

Cross-community dimension

The cross-community dimension is strongly in evidence. For the Lurgan Community Bridges Project, SPCA is in partnership with Mount Zion Community, seeking to promote cooperation and understanding across the religious and political divide. Shared community events, joint celebrations and courses have formed new friendships. The PAKT project has been running since 1993. Currently the 140 families mentioned above are drawn in equal numbers from both sides of the community. The project brings them closely together in a daily programme for 200 children and their parents. The children can engage in gymnastics, soccer, dancing, choir, drama, crafts, swimming lessons, computer tuition and a homework club, all of which are led by qualified teachers and tutors. For parents there are opportunities to learn new skills and for the family together there are days out, rambles, swimming sessions, barbecues and a residential weekend.

The Shankill Seniors' Group, in partnership with the Upper Bann Institute for Further and Higher Education, sets out to engage women and men over fifty years of age in an educational and social programme that makes all sections of the community feel welcome. The Cedars activity centre has over 200 members. A 'Dark Horse' award scheme encourages members to discover new talent within themselves and to pursue it for 100 hours over a period of at least 12 months. A Friendship Centre offers a relaxed meeting for 40 - 50 members each Monday afternoon and The Palms day centre provides a caring environment for more dependent elderly people on two days each week.

Further information appears in case study 2, page 76.

PROFILE 8: A METHODIST CONGREGATION, CITY MISSION, LONDONDERRY

Type

Methodist City Mission is a congregation established in the late nineteenth century in Waterside, Londonderry. On this the eastern side of the river Foyle there is an overall Protestant majority, but the wards are mixed, with several having a Catholic majority - in one case of 84 percent.

Objectives

The main objective of this FBO, as the minister expressed it, is to 'put faith into action as a servant church'. He saw this in terms of forging alliances with, and offering space to, community groups and others addressing issues of division and trying to create better circumstances for local people.

Activities

The congregation meet for worship each Sunday, with volunteers taking their place in the choir, or leading classes in the Sunday school or children's church. There is a micro class for eight to ten year olds and a youth fellowship for teenagers. During the week some members gather for Bible study or for a prayer meeting, young people for the Explorers group or the Girls' Brigade company. A group of senior citizens come together for a meal once a week and a hostel offers shelter for homeless men in the city. A church minibus is available for the use of these groups.

Buildings

The congregation's base is Clooney Hall, a purpose-built multi-functional building incorporating a reception area, multi-purpose hall, a range of meeting rooms and administrative offices, a coffee shop, worship centre and a six office suite for rental. The building stands at the interface between a majority Catholic and a majority Protestant ward of the town sector sketched above. The house for the minister and his family is within easy reach.

Section 3 Profiles of Twelve Faith-based Organisations   57

Participation

The congregation has over 200 members. There are 45 children in the Sunday school and 80 girls in the Girls' Brigade. About 70 senior citizens are served the weekly meal. Out of the 10 staff posts at Clooney Hall, 7 are filled, including that of centre manager. The amenities on offer in May 2001 attracted a daily weekday figure in the range of 259 to 403 people passing through the centre. The hostel for homeless men employs 18 staff members. The level of local ownership is high, with a mix of groups using the new building. The management committee is made up of representatives of the congregation and the user groups.

Resourcing and use of research

Grants towards the new building were received from the Community Relations Unit and from the Rank Trust. Derry City Council makes a contribution towards the salary for the manager's post. Rent from Foyle Trust as anchor tenants in the office suite and income from the coffee shop help keep the operation viable. The Methodist Church in Ireland does not accept income from gambling including the National Lottery. A major effort went into raising funds within the membership. In assessing the parameters of need in the locality this church had the benefit of an existing community and business audit prepared by the University of Ulster for the Waterside Area Partnership. In addition the proposal for the new centre built upon information drawn from a wide range of sources and interest groups to ensure that the congregation's hopes and plans fitted in with existing strategies for the area.

Linkages

There are links with Derry City Council, Foyle Trust, Northern Ireland Housing Executive, North and West Housing, the police Community Safety Team, Macmillan Cancer Relief, Relate, Partnership Care West, Resource Centre Derry, Stepping Stones Nursery, Age Concern, and with local churches and various community, social and recreational groups.

Cross-community dimension

Derry City Council, in a partnership with this church, provides some funding for staff. The community relations officer is involved in decisions about the use and management of the centre to help ensure that work and activity are of a cross-community nature. Some local statutory services for children are based in the centre. North West Community Support Partnership comprises City Mission, Foyle Trust and Resource Centre, Shantallow. This Partnership has brought a cross-community dimension to the provision of family support services in a new family centre at Clooney Hall. In these ways the organisation actively seeks opportunities to contribute to community through engagement in work that has relevance to everyone in the locality, regardless of their religious background.

PROFILE 9: A METHODIST BASED TRUST, BARNABAS, ENNISKILLEN

Type

The Barnabas Trust, incorporated as a trust in 1990, is located in Enniskillen, a county town of about 12,000 people in the south west of the province. This FBO originated as a community care programme within a Methodist congregation in the 1980s, as members responded to the perceived needs of elderly and isolated people in the town and surrounding area. It now involves the four main churches through its Inter Church Council of Representation.

Objectives

The main objective of the trust is given as 'social service as an expression of concern and compassion in the name of Jesus Christ and His Church'.

Activities

Social service is provided both by volunteers and by those who are paid through Work Track or New Deal arrangements. A team of community visitors trained to NVQ L2 in domiciliary care have established supportive links with people living alone within a ten to twelve mile radius of Enniskillen, who are cut off from society by age or infirmity. They have been instrumental in the installation of 'Lifeline' telephone systems and smoke alarms in many homes and in the distribution of surplus EC food. A team of decorators and gardeners provides assistance with the maintenance of houses and gardens where elderly residents can no longer look after the upkeep of their homes. The Trust's minibus is used to deliver community services and to bring people together, especially those with mobility problems, for education and recreation. A catering team produces affordable lunches each day in the Trust's restaurant and supports the leaders who facilitate recreation and craftwork for the groups for elderly people. A support group for mothers, with a crèche for their children, meets weekly to share problems and develop options for solutions. A special needs playgroup is open three mornings each week for referred children. Staff are trained to NVQ L2 child care. A programme for young people, devised in cooperation with them, is based in the centre's dry bar. A full-time youth worker's post has been frozen and three volunteers in residence at the centre facilitate a range of activities providing opportunity for self-development, recreation, training and work experience.

Buildings

Facilities are concentrated in a purpose-built centre that is physically linked to the Methodist church building next door. In addition to reception, day room and office suite, there is a basement dedicated to work with young people. Dormitories allow for residential courses, for visiting groups and for young people on 1 year placements through the international Youth For Christ programme.

Participation

There is a staff complement of 20 and a fluctuating band of volunteers. A catering team of eight prepares some 125 meals each week. Local involvement by young people and uptake of services has been encouraging, but the director felt that ownership could be stronger. At its peak Barnabas provided work and training opportunities for long-term unemployed people through Action for Community Employment (ACE), Community Work Programme, Community Volunteering Scheme and other schemes. The original eighteen staff, financed by the Training and Employment Agency, expanded by an additional 88 funded through the ACE scheme.

Resourcing and use of research

The raising of £300,000 in the 1990s to develop a new base was the result of some expertise in accessing funding sources. 'Various charitable trusts' and the International Fund for Ireland contributed around two thirds of this amount. The climate has changed however and the loss of ACE funding following the discontinuation by the government of this scheme has had a significant negative impact not only on the viability of the FBO itself, but upon the work with unemployed people and upon the level of trust that had been built up with socially excluded groups and individuals. Research energy is currently going into the search for long term funding.

Linkages

Informal contacts exist with statutory services, with churches in the area and with schools. Local medical practitioners are amongst those making referrals to the services on offer. There are no current partnerships or formal linkages between Barnabas and other organisations though the trust has contracts with Sperrin Lakeland Health and & Social Care Trust. There are long standing working relationships with Salvation Army, St Michael's parish, The Graan Abbey, St Vincent de Paul, NI Mental Health, 'Women Making Waves', MS Fermanagh branch, Enniskillen Youth For Christ and others. What the director called the 'meaningful link' is with the local Methodist Circuit and, through it, with the rural area surrounding the town.

Cross-community dimension

A cross-community dimension runs through all the Trust's activities. Though this FBO is Methodist in origin, records show times when over 40 percent of the client group and 60 percent of the staff group have been Catholic. Its trustees are drawn from all the churches. Its services, aimed at greatest need, are not confined to any one group. Its employees have been drawn from varied backgrounds.

PROFILE 10: A CROSS-DENOMINATIONAL ASSOCIATION, YMCA (NATIONAL COUNCIL), BELFAST

Type

National Council of YMCAs Ireland Ltd is the official name of YMCA Ireland, an all Ireland faith-based charitable organisation, created in 1981 by YMCA local associations. YMCA (National Council) describes itself as a cross-denominational youth movement committed to Christian social action in local communities. The executive committee is made up of representatives of local associations.

Objectives

The Memorandum and Articles of the National Council, setting out the objects for which it is established and detailing the powers it has in its pursuit of those objects, run to several pages. The strategic plan, adopted in 2000, states that the organisation's vision is 'to create learning situations for young people where they can develop physically, socially and spiritually, participating as co-creators in our shared community'. According to the mission statement, National Council exists to share the vision:

- by supporting and developing local associations as they engage in action in response to local youth and community need;
- by promoting partnership within the movement and;
- by assuring a quality approach (good practice) throughout the YMCA movement.

Activities

National Council, through its local work, its international linkages and liaison with outside bodies, performs a role that embraces the following areas. It supports the development of quality youth work at local association level by giving guidance, supporting agreed standards and working in partnership with local groups. It maintains and develops policies that support the values and activities of the movement and that promote unity within it. It represents the movement nationally, advocating for local associations with government and other national bodies. It acts as a bridge with the wider YMCA family including the European and World Alliances. National Council's main activities involve it in direct managerial support of local YMCAs and in curriculum support. There are 22 local YMCA groups, 13 of them in Northern Ireland, engaged in a wide range of activities within a curriculum that includes community relations, health promotion, family youth work, outdoor education and vocational training.

Buildings

National Council owns an outdoor education centre at Newcastle, County Down and leases 8 other sets of buildings. At local level the YMCA has ownership of approximately 13 buildings with a rough value of 5 million GBP in towns and cities across Ireland.

Participation

National Council employs 35 permanent and 25 temporary staff. It has about 120 volunteers. The movement has approximately 350 volunteers across the 22 local associations. Some 8,500 young people aged between 7 and 25 years are enrolled in the 13 local associations in Northern Ireland. Over the whole island of Ireland the organisation involves more than 38,300 people.

Resourcing and use of research

National Council is funded mainly by government and trust funding. Government sources contribute 61 percent, trust funds 23 percent and the rest comes from Council's own resources and fundraising effort. Local resourcing follows a similar pattern with perhaps greater emphasis on local fundraising.

The organisation, both centrally and locally, operates on a 'needs based concept' so most work is preceded by a needs analysis process. This can involve door-to-door research within the local community, data analysis and interviews with local agencies. It may be carried out within house or it may involve external consultants in evaluation exercises instigated either by Council or by a funding body. For example the Department of Education recently completed a year long inspection of the organisation and this study draws upon its report (Education and Training Inspectorate, 2002). Local units have adopted an evaluation policy that requires them to enlist the support of external evaluators for specific projects.

Linkages

Local programmes work in close collaboration with local community groups and sponsoring churches. Individual partnerships may be programme specific as in cross- border links in vocational training. On a broader scale YMCA works in partnership with larger agencies like Youth Action and is active in umbrella organisations like Youthnet and the National Youth Council of Ireland.

Cross-community dimension

Equity, diversity and interdependence (EDI) have been adopted as key values and included in the National Standards scheme. A senior staff member is dedicated to cross-community work. The worker role is to promote equity, diversity and interdependence in all local contexts. This generally means sectarianism in the north and racism in the south. The role helps focus on building EDI values into all programmes, for example work with non-nationals (asylum seekers in the Republic). Virtually all local YMCAs are engaged in community relations programmes and most have a strategy to recruit a diverse management committee.

PROFILE 11: A NEW CHURCH COMPANY, OASIS CARE, BELFAST

Type

Oasis has been a limited company with a board of directors since 1997. It grew out of the Christian Fellowship Church, a congregation within the new church movement situated on the edge of a predominantly Protestant eastern inner city area of Belfast.

Objectives

The mission statement presents Oasis as aiming to empower unemployed people and build up the life of families.

Activities

For long-term unemployed people opportunities are provided for developing job search skills, interview skills and CV preparation. There are accredited training courses designed to provide stepping stones to work. The focus on family is seen in facilities like the community café, drop-in centre with a crèche and a children's used clothes shop. Free child care allows women to consider enrolling for courses in personal development including health, home making, social skills, education and work. A parenting course is accredited through the Open College Network. A playgroup, formerly run at the centre by NSPCC, has been taken over by Oasis and an after school art club opens every weekday in school holidays.

With the support of the Probation Board, there is a drop-in facility for young people who are, or have been, on probation. A trainer is available to provide initial guidance for any caller with a problem of basic literacy or numeracy. The centre provides a space for band rehearsals and an arts-based cross-community experiment links this project with a community group in a Catholic enclave across the city.

A befriending scheme has been set up to help local people suffering from mental health problems. This pilot project employs a team of six staff under the Worktrack programme who take referrals from eight GP practices in the area.

Buildings

The organisation's base is a renovated and refurbished former public house, which includes café, drop-in, shop, two training rooms, computer suite and administrative offices.

Participation

The programmes occupy 12 members of staff, a core pool of 17 volunteers and 15 Worktrack employees. There is a high level of local ownership of and input into both design and implementation of projects. The centre is recognised for the delivery and assessment of national vocational qualifications (NVQs). One hundred and seventy five people have been trained through the government New Deal programme. Seventy six people have qualified in computer skills at various levels including the European Computer Driving Licence (ECDL). Forty eight women have gained Open College Network certificates in a range of topics, nine have won the Welcome Host Certificate from the Northern Ireland Tourist Board. A typical summer scheme caters for perhaps ninety children from 6 to 11 years old, with the staff team including international volunteers.

Resourcing and use of research

Funding, technical support and advice have come from BBC Children in Need, Belfast City Council, Belfast European Partnership Board, Belfast Regeneration Office, Business in the Community, Christian Fellowship Church, the Department of Education for Northern Ireland, the Educational Guidance Service for Adults, the Ford Foundation, International Fund for Ireland, the Probation Board for Northern Ireland, the Training and Employment Agency, the Training for Women Network, the local Health and Social Services Trust among other bodies. Contracts are entered into with each funding body. Research has underpinned each stage of this FBO's development. From the first area survey to find out what the main issues were for local people, through door-to-door conversations about developing a community resource, the organisation built up local knowledge and made use of it to identify possible responses. Further research took it into dialogue with statutory bodies and with other community groups in the area. Oasis looked

Section 3 Profiles of Twelve Faith-based Organisations   65

elsewhere at church-based action in cities like London and Liverpool and saw good practice from which to learn. It took up offers of practical help from people working in successful faith-based social action projects in England and, through Training into Jobs, gained insight into financial issues and learned how to make grant applications. The pilot befriending scheme, for example, came about through a combination of awareness of local conditions, contact with professionals concerned about them, and in joint response to mental health needs clearly identified through research studies elsewhere in Belfast.

Linkages

Local links are in place with the Greater East Belfast Partnership, East Belfast Business Initiative, East Belfast Community Development Agency, East Belfast Churches Forum. Collaborative relationships have been established with community organisations in Canada and in the United States. This FBO in partnership with two local organisations offers 27 training places on the Microsoft Certified Professional Level in IT skills.

Cross-community dimension

Creative links also cross the community divide. Twenty week visual arts modules for young people have been designed to combat sectarianism. Through residential cross-community workshops and the public performances and exhibitions with which the modules have ended, relationships have been built and sustained beyond the structured experience. For women, short residentials in Dublin with exchange visits to Belfast have helped overcome difference and preconceptions.

Further information appears in case study 4, page 84.

PROFILE 12: AN UNAFFILIATED COMPANY, MORNINGTON COMMUNITY PROJECT, BELFAST

Type

Mornington is a faith-based voluntary association that takes the form of a limited company with a board, director and management team and has been in existence just over twelve years. It is located in the lower Ormeau area of south Belfast, a once religiously mixed neighbourhood that is now predominantly Catholic. It has no formal connection with, or basis in, any church.

Objectives

The organisation describes itself as 'a project working with the community to build a better community'.

Activities

The core of the operation is employment training and provision of work experience. It also offers a variety of services from home and environmental improvement through recreational and social activities for older people to events and educational opportunities for local people of all ages. In addition it provides a range of parent and child related groups as well as a youth club, a community restaurant and a drop-in centre for information exchange.

Buildings

Based in three storey premises in an unprepossessing terrace, its 'store front' café presents a welcoming public face to the main thoroughfare.

Participation

There are 3 full-time staff, with 3 temporary staff on employment schemes. Mornington draws on 79 volunteers, some of them highly skilled, in diverse roles. It also employs 2 young adults from overseas on one-year placements from Youth For Christ, an international religious agency. At present there are 138 people involved in information technology or job search training, all with an eye to evolving employment possibilities in the immediate area. Currently 18 families use the mother and toddler group. There are 25 children in the after schools project, 120 members of the children's club and 35 young people in the youth club. The women's group has 45 local participants. The level of local ownership is high.

Resourcing and use of research

Ability to access grants has become a critical issue. Until 1996, the balance of funding was 70 percent government, 30 percent trust funds. With a change in government policy on funding has come greater dependence on trusts and on sympathetic individuals. The balance of funding is now roughly trust funds 45 percent, individuals 25 percent, government (e.g. employment training) and European sources 30 percent. Research into the local training and employment market was carried out for Mornington by Community and Technical Aid. Less formal research in the sense of ongoing dialogue with local people has shaped its responses to disadvantage as it is experienced in the area and has led to co-operative relationships with other agencies.

Linkages

This FBO has entered into partnerships and cooperative linkages with a large and diverse range of community, voluntary, statutory and private agencies to share and combine knowledge and practice to address the needs of disadvantaged people. The agencies have included health trusts, the Training and Employment Agency, a university society, a Belfast Partnership, local and regional business groups. The ventures have ranged from drawing up community development strategies, developing community businesses, addressing the needs of those who are designated 'unemployable', providing guidance in Christian community development thinking and practice and establishing cross-community employment projects.

Cross-community dimension

The cross-community dimension finds explicit expression in the religiously mixed nature of the management team. Mornington aims to model cross-community cooperation. A sustained attempt to promote increased understanding between Protestant and Catholic people runs through the whole range of its activity and involves 150 people at any one time. It is specifically focused in a faith development education module, engaging 25 people, designed in response to suggestions from local people.

Further information appears in case study 5, page 91.

SECTION 4 CASE STUDIES OF FIVE FAITH-BASED ORGANISATIONS

The section sets out five case studies which, in trying to communicate something of the flavour and 'feel' of some aspects of what are very different organisations, follow a less uniform style than that of the profiles.

CASE 1: 'BENMOE'S 'SHEBEG' PASTORAL CENTRE, 'BALLYCARN'

I push the bell and wait at the door. Virtually every window in this twelve flat housing block is shuttered. All the buildings around are grey in colour. The street lights in the immediate vicinity are fitted with floodlights at the top of the lamp posts and closed circuit cameras are in evidence. There is no human being in sight. *It is difficult, but we are in here and it will change us.* **The minister's words come to mind and I begin to sense something of what he meant. A remote voice checks me. The door lock is released. Inside the paint is fresh, the rooms clean, the staff welcoming, but there are grilles and alarms on the windows. This is 'Shebeg' Pastoral Centre on a weekday morning, a drop-in centre demanding more than passing curiosity to enter.**

Lara, the community worker, admitted that the heavy security was a challenge, a big psychological barrier. She added that it was just part of what has to be accepted for the moment. A detached house would make a better base. There are none on the estate. Taking over a semi would present noise problems to neighbours. She saw it as part of a kind of test. In post for two years, she became a familiar figure in her first six months on foot around the estate, knocking on doors, getting to know local people, talking to anyone and everyone. She listened to them, matching her own abilities and ideas to their views.

Even then, when the pastoral centre opened in November 2000, there was local scepticism. People wondered if there would be police at the drop-in, or the drug squad, or social workers - somebody to check up on them. This was one of the roots of a sense of being tested that she and the volunteers staffing the centre shared. Another was an intuition that they had to earn people's trust. She recounted how, when the interior of the block was being refurbished, a band of

Section 4 Case Studies of Five Faith-based Organisations 69

local children, aged between seven and nine, let down the tyres of the contractors' vans. The men rushed outside and the children entered the building and stole tools and keys. They repeated the trick on a later occasion, this time leaving a window unlocked for entry by night. Another element of the testing came with teenagers dropping shotgun cartridges at the feet of the centre volunteers. At a time when the estate was becoming more Catholic, when there were some very angry and aggressive Protestant people around and when paramilitary organisations were actively recruiting amongst young people in the area this was frightening enough.

There was no surprise at the early scepticism they encountered. In Lara's view, people's experience teaches them to look for the catch if there appears to be something going for nothing. They become disillusioned and fed up with others doing things to them or for them. They want a part in the decisions.

> ***Consultation at every step is necessary. We check the programme with the residents' association. We try to be open, honest and listening. We take time with individual people. If we don't do it that way we might as well shut up shop*** (Respondent 2).

The programme at the centre is implemented by Lara and her team of eighteen volunteers. They keep the drop-in open on weekday mornings, providing support for young mothers specifically on Wednesdays. They facilitate a faith formation group and a homework club. The evening programme involves them in work with 15-19 year olds and with a group for girls. Such young people, some with very troubled backgrounds, slowly came to realise that the centre staff would not collude with the lawbreaking that is part of their culture, but would treat them with honesty and listen to what they might want to say about how they see the world they live in. This is a demanding process and the volunteers have to be carefully selected for the work. They are at the sharp edge of Benmoe Presbyterian congregation's millennium project entitled 'Investing in Community', an effort to change life on one of the four estates they see as their patch.

The congregation put in the financial resources to renovate the centre. They pay the nominal rent and employ the worker. They also supply the volunteers and, not least, the moral support for the operation. That support has a practical edge. Six weeks after the centre opened they reviewed working arrangements and made adjustments because of the sense of volunteers being at risk. One member of the congregational committee managing the centre expressed his concerns as follows:

> ***The volunteers who are accepted are usually not people with answers, but those with injuries who can in some sense say 'we***

> *know about this'. They are our most valuable resource. We need to find some way of supporting them better. We are not just doing our own wee thing for people through the community worker and leaving it all to her and the volunteers. We are trying to engage and to enable local people to emerge in leadership positions in the area* (Respondent 3).

A member of the congregation who no longer lives in the area confessed to being a little nervous of the estate on which the work is being developed. Yet he was also convinced of the rightness of the principle of serving the local community and the need for the church to do something, without being sure that this was the only or best way to go about it. He was uncertain about how far the venture should be shared with other faith communities and unclear about how far it should ever bend to fit a government agenda in order to procure funding. He wondered whether the pastoral centre itself should not be more obviously Christian looking. Those who staff it tend to think that this could frighten people off. They do not want faith to be 'in your face when you come through the door. We have to earn the right to share Christ with people'. To keep the congregation's interest alive and informed Lara gave a series of Sunday morning presentations on the project in order to offer her understanding that care has to be non patronising and practical.

Such thoughts seemed broadly in line with the minister's approach. Daniel describes himself as being conservative in theology. Certain aspects of his thinking have particular significance within this setting. The first of these is his model of the church as present and down to earth, not distant and formal, its purpose not primarily to lead or direct but, as he put it, 'to serve as Christ was servant king'. Following from this, he encourages a sense of a call to the whole congregation to be servants in the locality. For this to be authentic they must first look and listen. They must recognise that life for many in the area is a struggle and that the church is itself in a position of weakness. It was his own looking and listening, his interpretation of the changing demography of the area and the resulting questions, that led Daniel to suggest to his kirk session that they find a community worker for the patch instead of simply taking another assistant minister for a brief period of training.

A second significant aspect of the leader's approach is the willingness to cooperate with any who share a concern or a responsibility for the locality. Benmoe congregation, along with four other local churches, is an associate member of the local partnership. Through this partnership they have developed extensive local links with police, education and youth services, with a range of charitable bodies, local councillors and residents' associations. The pastoral centre is located in the block of flats that the partnership took over from the housing executive to service community groups. As Daniel says,

> *willingness to work together is the key thing and we are now seen as no longer working for ourselves alone, so the barriers have begun to fall. People just didn't know about resources in the church for the community.*

A third important dimension in the leader's thinking relates to those very resources. As Daniel describes it,

> *the church can operate as a hospital and as an army. You can come and be cared for. You can go on from there to a position of sacrificial living. A significant number of our people are at that stage. It is an individual thing and it is entirely voluntary. From such members our resources are gifted rather than requested.*

Thus no external funding has been sought by this church and this is likely to continue while the base for the pastoral centre remains available at the current rent. The organisation is motivated by what members see as a response to a scriptural imperative and this rules out being deflected from its course by the demands of any funder.

This scriptural imperative and basis is given expression in the congregation's framework for mission, drafted as part of the 'Investing in Community' project. The framework traces a line from this basis to the cutting edge of the work, the quality of relationship on offer at the pastoral centre and the attitude and demeanour of the volunteers there. On the way it emphasises the fundamental value of human beings and the specific needs of people in the immediate neighbourhood. It underlines the necessity for the local faith community to address those needs in cooperation with other concerned individuals and groups in society. It places the pastoral centre and its workers at the heart of this enterprise, acknowledging it as a learning experience for all involved. Certain principles are added to guide the work along humane and inclusive lines. Three headings from what is virtually a declaration of intent and rationale for the whole operation provide some insight into the philosophy.

> *Volunteers: Our volunteers are the most valuable resource in the centre. Their opinions and needs must be valued and a high priority given to the development of our volunteers.*
> *Community Development: In prioritising work load, those things most likely to contribute to community development will be a major consideration.*
> *Partnership: The primary function of 'Benmoe' Presbyterian Church is to be a church. We recognise the valuable contributions that many other agencies make to helping the local community. In working alongside them we seek neither to usurp nor duplicate what others are doing. In this way we therefore make best use of the resources made available to 'Shebeg' Pastoral Centre by the Church Committee.* (Framework for Mission - May 2001)

This is a neighbourhood with a Presbyterian church and a Catholic school situated just across the road from each other and contact between them has apparently been limited to one event in the last twenty five years. A Catholic church in another part of the town has been the focus of a turbulent Protestant picket. There is fear. A kind of renewed ghettoisation is under way along with what was termed 'a push in paramilitary muscle'. Any perceived lack of progress in the political process heightens anger and frustration amongst such groups, ratcheting up tension and cramping room for manoeuvre. There is the feeling that a major incident might 'split things'. Someone commented, 'If it breaks down I've got to watch my back'. It is not a context that encourages risk taking. Certain kinds of cooperation are not well received by paramilitary bodies.

Yet there is a cross-community dimension to the organisation's work, 'focused in activity below the line of sight'. Some initiatives, like networking, have been quietly progressing. Lara has developed strong working links right across the spectrum. The groups at the pastoral centre accept anyone who comes to the door and they represent what is termed 'a good spread'. The faith formation group is referred to as 'a big mix', involving church folk plus charismatic Catholics. Daniel meets regularly with other clergy in the area. There is an interdenominational monthly meeting of people drawn from the local churches to which information from the clergy fraternal is fed through. There is a determination that life is not to be dictated by sectarianism.

Within such a setting of division, anecdotal feedback from people reinforces the sense that perceptions are changing. One long term resident remarked on the dramatic improvement in the residents' association, the renewed sense of pride and a recent action taken in the face of the greatest paramilitary pressure he had seen in twenty years. In a clean up on the estate the people almost defiantly reclaimed the streets, clearing them of rubbish and graffiti and washing kerbs. He also noted a new concern about peacemaking, now legitimate where previously it had been considered to be simply a Republican agenda.

There was the community carol service which would ordinarily have attracted church members only but which, in the light of a rejuvenated community association and the new element of cooperation, was massively supported. Organised by the partnership group, the residents' association and the senior citizens' club, the event was advertised in the residents' association newsletter as a cross-community church service. It was the first move in cross-community work where the local clergy were seen 'above the line of sight'. The size and spirit of the gathering surprised local people and strengthened the desire for a renewed sense of community and belonging.

Barriers seem to have been broken down through the local partnership. When the churches made a submission to the partnership applying for the use of the flat as a pastoral centre they received a positive response. The fact that churches are seen to be making an effort to listen to each other and to the language and thinking of local people has opened new doors. The partnership grew out of a need to address local issues at a time when community spirit was in steep decline.

The existing local groups, including the churches, were too weak to combat the decline on their own. The clergy, wondering how best to respond, began to meet with each other regularly in order to begin to find a common way forward on social issues. Associate membership of the partnership followed. At their regular meetings a project is taking shape that could begin to make a contribution to the battle with interlocking sectarianism and drug-related deprivation. On one of the estates where the Housing Executive has been knocking down homes (because it was said that few people wanted to live there) the churches are planning to take some land and build new homes for owner occupation through Habitat for Humanity. This will involve them in an exercise of community building so that potential buyers will have the confidence that this is a good place to live.

As described by the interviewees, this work is not about quantification or target setting. It is about building trust between people and raising their hope that things can be better. It is perhaps to be measured only in small ways. At the church building the fact that there is little vandalism may be indicative of a process under way. At the pastoral centre there is the beginning of a similar sense of ownership. People who drop in there feel comfortable enough to make their own cup of tea and to talk with some openness because they know that what they think counts to the team there.

The community worker provides a regular report with some statistics for the management committee. But, as one voice said,

> *You can't quantify, it's not like a job centre. You can list people's practical problems, but the more personal matters that are talked about, you can't talk about, you have to take care. How do you put a value on the opportunity for people just to come in and sit down for some human warmth while a volunteer takes care of the youngster for a while? The missionaries back from Malawi can give a glowing account to the congregation, but you can't talk much about what happens on your doorstep. Somebody somewhere will be able to work out who and what you are talking about. What are on offer here are respect, time and honesty. Life stories are told, trust fostered. You can't measure the therapeutic value of an ear. On Monday night the kids benefit, but so does the whole estate, and their parents. And there is the satisfaction of knowing that you were the first place they called to talk after they had been in a situation* (Respondent 2).

In the light of Lara's first 2 year contract the job specification for the community and youth worker post was redrawn. The first document provided a 14 point list of what it called 'duties'. Of these 8 relate to conventional work with congregation based young people and 6 to encouraging links between congregation and community. There is clearly an implicit hope of adding to the membership of the church. One duty stands apart, namely 'to evaluate and report on the needs of people living in the local community'.

The revised specification is a different kind of document. It speaks of responsibilities rather than duties and the focus of these is more outward looking to the people of the neighbourhood than to the congregation. They revolve around the running of the pastoral centre; the recruitment, encouragement and organisation of volunteers; promoting the facilities of the centre locally; liaising with other church groups or individuals with a community interest to encourage

Section 4 Case Studies of Five Faith-based Organisations 75

them to use the centre; seeking and taking opportunity to work alongside other community based organisations; taking initiatives to address gaps in community provision - amongst others.

These two specifications relate to a job that came into being because the minister of this congregation did not take the usual path and look for an assistant equipped for traditional ministry in the church. He began to ask himself fundamental questions about the nature of the task facing his organisation in his locality. He shared his thinking with other members. Together they opened themselves to learning from and working with other individuals and groups who, while not necessarily pursuing the same questions, had similar concerns. Their actions and their attitudes slowly became clear to those around them and caught the interest and the trust of a significant number of local people and agencies. The difference between the two job specification documents is a clear indication of the congregation's growing understanding of the task it has taken on in its millennium project and of how it is itself changing as it seeks to bring about change.

CASE 2: SHANKILL'S JETHRO PROJECT, LURGAN

Who is Jethro? The story is about Moses, a leader of God's people who was admonished by his father-in-law, Jethro, for trying to do all the work of ministry himself and as a result was burning himself out and was frustrating the people by not getting all the work done satisfactorily. On the Lord's behalf, Jethro commands Moses to adopt a radically different pattern of ministry. Moses is told to find suitable people who would take on responsibilities of leadership and who would share the heavy load with him. These people, in turn, would have others assisting them so that the work that needed to be done, instead of being focused on just one man would be accomplished efficiently by a large number of people. (From 'The Rector Writes' in Focus, 2000).

Shankill is a parish in transition and not simply because of its recent change of minister. Before then the traditional pattern of ministry, focused in a single ordained person, was being augmented by a dispersed and shared ministry acknowledged within the organisation as an integral part of everyone's membership. This was promoted over the previous decade as the 'Jethro principle'. The result is the development of a culture of expectation that every member has something to offer and would be willing to give time and energy to the work of the congregation. This culture is further strengthened by a training course (Network) designed to help members discover what they might be capable of offering to the mission. In this way the organisation produces a body of volunteers large enough to resource the range of activities outlined in the profile above.

> *I am fully convinced that ministry, as we find it in the New Testament, is all about mobilising every member of the church to use the gifts God has given them. This is key. It is not just about an active ordained person ministering to a large number of passive lay people. It is about each member of the Christian body discovering what their part to play is and then playing it wholeheartedly* (Respondent 1).

Section 4 Case Studies of Five Faith-based Organisations

The process of discovering a part to play is encouraged amongst individual members within the organisation. It is also pursued by the organisation itself, as the members increasingly come to see their church as part of the larger society in Lurgan. Churches change only slowly, but questions about what the church is for and what belonging to it means were triggered by tension between the two main religious identities and political affiliations in the town as they responded to the outworking of the political process following the Belfast Agreement in 1998. These questions are actively addressed through the communication channels and networks that are part of the life of any parish. Religion as a controlling and exclusive dimension to life is ruled out. Religion as a vehicle for building community and promoting basic social values has been embraced by the parish. The result is an outward looking vision, incorporating an intention to put the resources of the organisation at the service of the local community.

This is the task for which the congregation's voluntary community development organisation, the Shankill Parish Caring Association, was formed. It has a remit to advance education and to provide facilities in the interests of social welfare without distinction of age, sex, race, political, religious, or other opinion. Where those facilities are wanting, the aim is to make them better. It is the specific aim of 'Jethro' to bring together all who want to make such facilities better.

The whole thrust of the Jethro Project is to provide the best possible resource through which the Shankill members may join with others and exercise their voluntary ministry in the service of the community. Over the past decade church premises have become a major focus for community activity. Some 45,000 people of all backgrounds were estimated to use services and programmes in the existing buildings. Having clearly identified the potential for growth to meet further emerging needs, this congregation through its Caring Association now puts energy and imagination into a project designed to enhance the lives and the prospects of all who live in and beyond the town. The aim is to establish a new community-focused social resource centre in place of the complex of buildings that has existed since the 1960s. At the new centre, more people will be enabled to improve their skills and competencies and thus become more employable. In this way the self-confidence and capability of the community will be built up.

Partnership agreements and close working relationships between the Caring Association and a range of statutory bodies have been in place for some time, as noted in the profile. A track record of cooperative working and good management practice has been established. So when the involvement of the local Council was sought in determining a way forward for the project, a formal partnership was readily agreed. A project Steering Group was then set up to include the Shankill Parish Caring Association, Craigavon Borough Council, Shankill Parish Select Vestry, Southern Education and Library Board, Craigavon and Banbridge Community Health and Social Services Trust and the local Primary School. The Group commissioned a professional economic appraisal of the proposed facility and this was completed in 2001. It is noteworthy that social as well as purely economic objectives were taken into consideration in this exercise.

An exhaustive listing of Shankill parish activity is provided in profile 7. However it is worth recalling here the groups that make use of the buildings occupying the site of the proposed Jethro Centre:- The Cedars (a group for active elderly people); The Palms (a group for people suffering from dementia and who may also be physically disabled); The Friendship Centre (a seniors' recreation group); Boys' Brigade, Girl Guides and Scouts (uniformed youth organisations); The Crusaders (a church youth group); The Buzz Youth Group; a Mother and Toddlers Club; Bowling Club; Badminton Club; Kids' Kingdom; Shankill Parish Church.

The envisaged centre aims to provide the following facilities.

- A hall for community use for bowls, badminton, concerts and occasional worship.
- A Youth Unit offering meeting spaces, coffee bar area, changing rooms and storage space for each youth organisation.
- An Early Childhood Unit containing two activity rooms, a secure outdoor play area, toilets and kitchen to provide child care services to users of the centre.
- A Seniors Unit with two activity rooms and a specialist bathroom facility suitable for elderly and disabled people.
- A General Purposes Area with a multi-purpose sports hall, coffee lounge and lobby with activity and meeting rooms.
- Office space for administrative needs.
- A floodlit outdoor recreational and sports area to accommodate a range of team sports and a garden area.

The analysis demonstrates how what the FBO is setting out to do is in keeping with the strategic aims of statutory bodies in the area and it reveals the potential of the Caring Association to make a contribution to their broad objectives. These include capacity building and community development; improving community relations; providing accessible facilities for welfare, education and recreation;

Section 4 Case Studies of Five Faith-based Organisations

making opportunity for employment training; promoting greater knowledge and understanding of differing cultural traditions; working at community reconciliation.

In order to clarify whether the proposed facility was needed to the extent that significant public money should be made available for its development, SPCA first focused attention on the tense community relations backcloth against which everyday life was lived. It noted that outbreaks of sporadic violence made people reluctant to frequent parts of the town, especially after dark, and gave parents cause for concern for their children when attending evening activities. The FBO's youth workers reported paramilitary and criminal elements encouraging young people into drug abuse and other anti-social activity. It then pointed to its close links with Mount Zion, a Roman Catholic community development organisation, with which it was already working by example and education to change the community relations atmosphere and develop community reconciliation in the town.

CASE 3: HOLY FAMILY CATHOLIC PARISH, BELFAST

What is a parish? It may be anything from two score homes in a village to several thousand in a wilderness of housing estates (...) But, whatever the scene within that arbitrary line on the map one thing remains the same. The line is there because it identifies people. (...) The whole purpose of the Parish system is to include people, all the people, to make sure that in the whole network of parishes all over the country everyone belongs somewhere. But in another sense a parish is not that at all. It is just a very few people who meet week by week in a building (...) the people who make up the parish in the narrow sense can never quite forget the larger community. After all they belong to that too (Baker, 1981 p. 43).

The line that marks the boundary of Holy Family Parish is a long and winding one. It runs from the tight streets around Duncairn Gardens in inner Belfast northwards to encompass the wider spaces of Parkmount and Fortwilliam, follows the North Circular Road, bulging to include the heights of Kilcoole and Sunningdale, then drops down the Cavehill Road to return to Newington. Along the way there are flashpoints where Protestant Loyalist territory is marked out. Here and there the bricked up terraces and occasional sightings of black amongst the plethora of more common flags serve as sharp and bleak reminders of the social deprivation, violence and paramilitary shadow against which everyday life is lived out.

Within the line there are 2,633 families, some 7,829 individual people, who are registered with the parish office as members of the parish as distinct from people who are not, or who may not be Catholic. There are networks of charity, of voluntary work and of the arts. And despite the effects of contemporary social and geographical mobility, people here retain a sense of place, of origin and of continuity.

One respondent, born in the area, explained how the parish is a focus of meaning and continuity for her. Speaking of the history of this part of Belfast which she has known all her life, she told of the expansion and growth of the parish, the decision to erect one and then a second church building in addition to the original church in Newington. This brought a natural tendency for people to begin to see the parish as three parts, with each church a focal point for members enjoying different standards of living or experiencing different pressures because of where they lived. She illustrated this with reference to evening social functions, how people who live in the relatively better off neighbourhoods can attend such events more easily than people who live near a flashpoint and who are understandably reluctant to leave their homes at night. She saw Holy Family, with these pressures to pull it apart, as a microcosm of Northern Ireland, with its tendency to fragmentation. Loyalty to the parish was encouraged in many different ways in order to hold diversity together. She described the bonding quality of this loyalty as developing

> ***a relationship with God through church, something that makes you want to give as well as get. There's a difference between loyalty to a job and loyalty to church. One is contractual, one voluntary. I say that though baptism is a contract too. Both have responsibilities. Holy Family is my faith family. It requires neighbourliness of me*** (Respondent 3).

The statement contains a passing reference to a fundamental Christian initiation ceremony, one of the ritual actions that function as powerful binding mechanisms and provide a sense of identity for members of a Catholic parish. The respondent understood herself as entering the 'faith family' by baptism. For this 'faith family' perhaps the central rite is the mass, or eucharist, from a Greek word meaning 'thanksgiving' in which the members of the parish come together in gratitude and worship, to be bonded as people of faith and strengthened for living out the 'neighbourliness' and the 'responsibilities' to which she referred.

Other religious rites also foster belonging and inclusion by encouraging the reconciliation of those who are alienated, building the relationship of those who are to be married and strengthening those whose marriage is in difficulty. Consolation, reassurance and the support of the parish community are offered through anointing in sickness and by means of a funeral liturgy at the time of death. In such ways, the people of the parish are bound together in a community that commands their loyalty.

At Holy Family, there are other ways too of reinforcing a sense of a shared undertaking. The necessary business of raising money provides an example. Everyone could have a part in the upkeep of the parish by contributing through the Sunday collection envelopes. Gifts were directed towards parochial, diocesan, national or international ends. There is a committee whose particular remit is to reduce the debt on the eighteen buildings for which the parish is responsible. Some 160 volunteer promoters cover every street in the parish, calling personally every week to collect contributions to a financial pool from which prizes are drawn. An average of £50,000 per year was being raised in this way at the beginning of 2002.

This involvement of volunteers, encouraged by the priests, extends to the daily running of the parish, in worship and in planning for the future. The parish team, made up of paid professionals, meets regularly for business each week. They work closely with the pastoral council, a group of volunteers who take an active role in the mission of the organisation and in working to develop a sense of the parish as a community. They meet monthly and go on annual retreat to think together about the lives that their people are living against a background of sectarian tension in the parish. They reflect upon ways of responding to events like marriage breakdown, bereavement, illness or unemployment, to the high suicide rate in the parish, and to conditions associated with drink and drug addiction or loneliness.

Through the interest groups run by the church there is an attempt to heighten people's awareness of the difficulties that marginalised or excluded people face. For example a friendship group brings together teachers and people with learning disabilities to develop their grasp of the faith. A support group for homosexual people meets regularly. People who were homebound can be included in Sunday worship through specially commissioned volunteers who bring the eucharist to their home from the church. They can also feel connected through the Sunday broadcast from church to radio receivers available from the parish office. The sense of belonging is further strengthened through use of the special family prayer book, printed and distributed to all parishioners, with a candle to light when saying prayers. A weekly bulletin also keeps people in touch, as does a parish magazine published twice each year. A special book was produced to mark the centenary of the parish (Carville, 1993).

This centenary book is telling in what it reveals of the strength of family identity, tradition and roots nurtured at Holy Family church. Contributions from long standing residents offer vivid memories of times past. They chart the growth of the parish tenfold from the early days when there were about a thousand parishioners, many of them in domestic service. They recount tales of fundraising efforts for the erection of three churches (opened 1895, 1937 and 1980) in place of the single original zinc building. They recall the building of the schools and their experience of specific teachers and fellow pupils. They marvel at how many of the family names of childhood days are still present in the parish, despite the forcible removal of families from their homes in the turbulent 1920s and the deaths, damage and evacuation of the 1941 blitz.

The book records the challenges that came with the Troubles and the near despair in the lives of almost every family at the lower end of the parish in the 1970s. Since that time two of the three churches in the parish have suffered more than one sectarian attack. The newest was severely damaged by a bomb shortly before its blessing and dedication ceremony was due to take place. What was seen as saving the area from total disintegration was the formation of a Residents' Committee involving cooperation with local Protestant ministers, representatives of residents, army and police.

There are messages from local Protestant ministers in the centenary book. These outline the ongoing contact between ministers from Presbyterian, Methodist, Moravian, Church of Ireland and Catholic churches in the area. They illustrate the cumulative value of regular meetings that build the trust to facilitate frank discussion and enable a measure of working together. Out of this has come several series of talks on issues facing all Christians, regular ecumenical services with a sharing of pulpits, a faith development programme run cooperatively by local churches and a joint pilgrimage to Iona. One message reads 'We have pledged ourselves to work together in a shared mission to express among ourselves God's love, peace and acceptance, and to bring this to bear on all the people across the divide in our shared, but broken, and yet single community of people who are called to owe our first allegiance to God in Christ' (Carville, 1993, p.78).

An example of the ordinary openness to be found in the parish is the day centre, running since 1978. Premises owned by the parish were made available for refurbishment by the Eastern Health Board to provide hairdressing, laundry, chiropody, restaurant, library, art and craft tuition and bathing facilities. It is open to all elderly people in the locality and run on an interdenominational basis. Voluntary helpers from the churches in the area are seen as the key to its success.

> *The parish is the most venerable of local institutions. Its history stretches back across the centuries; it is the depository of a people's traditions and religion and customs and sense of place. If, inevitably, the parish is in part museum, it is a living museum that knows how to make its historical artefacts work in the present. If it has the features of an organisation or institution, it knows how to make space for the individual and the personal and the idiosyncratic, and how to foster a community among them* (Sweeney, 2001 p.46).

CASE 4: OASIS FAMILY CENTRE, BELFAST

I follow Paul on the short twisting back street drive from the church. This part of inner east Belfast is looking run down and frayed. The tribal markings are Protestant, but more half hearted graffiti than triumphant full gable ends. Here and there a gap in the intermittently occupied terrace fronts gives on to a vista of rubble, tortured ground and caterpillar tracks as the way is made for new housing. The exposed clay strengthens an impression of shell shock in the air. We pull in at a corner building and bundle up narrow stairs past what seems like an army of workmen inside. Two floors up in a small quiet office I am handed over to Cliff. This is my introduction to Oasis Family Centre in the process of creation from a former paramilitary pub.

Paul is the pastor of the Christian Fellowship Church (CFC) congregation behind the Oasis initiative in East Belfast. Cliff is the centre manager. They and others pieced together the story behind the constructive chaos on the floors below. What is now up and running as a much used venue for a whole range of social, recreational and training activities was at the time of this field visit just coming into being. It was the congregation's third and most promising base for the work they felt they had to do. Broadly speaking, that work is seen as about establishing some mechanism through which local people can be put in touch with resources inside themselves, begin to realise their potential and change their lives and maybe their own neighbourhood for the better. The latest building offers greater scope than the two earlier ones occupied by the Oasis team.

They had first taken a house next to the church building as a base from which they could translate their sense of calling into practical and manageable action. There in 1993 they set up a drop-in centre, trained some volunteers to service it and waited. They were disappointed. Few people came to the house. Those who did turn up included a significant number of people with minor but troublesome mental health problems. The volunteers felt they were not equipped to cope with this sort of demand, so the house was closed and the church team began to think again.

Section 4 Case Studies of Five Faith-based Organisations

This had not been a total shot in the dark. The congregation had carried out a community audit to try to build some understanding of local need. In response to the picture it gave them they knew an advice centre of some kind would provide a starting point for their work and an accessible presence in the neighbourhood. But after the experience of the first house they believed they needed more focus and some guidance from those with knowledge of the area. They began to talk to professionals familiar with the area. They learned that teenage pregnancy rates were giving cause for concern. After discussions with Social Services the church began to offer support and encouragement to pregnant girls between the ages of thirteen and eighteen. A weekly drop-in club was run in the church house for about a year. The location was not ideal and they found the girls becoming, if anything, more dependent upon the support on offer than independent. They also identified a greater need among those aged eighteen to twenty, since younger women tended to be supported within the parental home on first giving birth. Those having a second child were often more isolated. In the light of these findings they began to look for a more suitable and strategically situated house within their target area - inner east Belfast.

After discussions the Housing Executive made a house available to the congregation in a location that suited their needs. The Executive contributed new kitchen facilities and church folk and ACE workers redecorated the house throughout. When they opened the door in February 1996 there was barely a discernible ripple of interest in the community despite the efforts they had made to promote it as a resource. Even the small group of women who showed initial curiosity seemed in danger of fading away and the church people were unsure about what to do. Their uncertainty came to an end when a key person, someone of influence within local networks, paid a visit to check out the atmosphere and talk to the volunteers. After that word seemed to get to the right ears. Women began to trickle in and to use the facilities offered by the house.

The question then was where, if anywhere, to take things from there. The volunteers drew the women into a conversation about how to make use of the resource and what activities they would find meaningful. They tried out a range of programmes, with uneven success. Eventually a parenting course was adapted to the local context. Nine months later response had grown to the point where so much more seemed possible, but lack of space in 'the wee house' was seriously limiting.

Meanwhile the group had also been sharpening its awareness of the impact of the high level of unemployment in the area. With the help of Making Belfast Work they carried out some research which showed them that, despite the existence of local ACE schemes, a growing number of families were feeling increasingly hopeless about their prospects. The question of what might be done to combat the malaise was pursued through dialogue with Social Services and with community groups in the area. They also talked to other churches in order to build connections and share ideas. This last was a slow process, confronting them with a dilemma. Were they to try to pull churches together first in order to attack the problems or get something off the ground and then talk to other churches about working cooperatively?

They opted to get something moving and went out to find examples of the kind of practice they felt could prove effective in their neighbourhood. They looked to the experience of faith-based organisations in other large UK cities. They found ready and practical help. One large established FBO employed a member of the CFC congregation and placed him formally in Belfast to move the Oasis project forward. Proposals now began to attract funding. The Probation Board of Northern Ireland provided some support. Money from the European Union's Peace Programme, 'peace money', became available and then the Educational Guidance Service for Adults funded two workers for two years.

The group now had ideas. They also had the staff and volunteers to implement them. Necessary support was in place and, not least, they had built up a level of credibility amongst people on the ground. But they lacked a more appropriate base in which all these elements could come together. They looked over a disused factory and considered putting in a bid. It was sold before they could secure the necessary finance. They explored the possibility of sharing other church premises in the area. Then 'The Farmers' Rest', a pub closed down by police because of paramilitary connections and subsequently the site of a failed business enterprise, came on the market. They bought the building and began to renovate and occupy it piecemeal as money became available.

The larger building became a successful base for the range of activities drawn up through ongoing consultation between the FBO and potential users. The rooms were decorated in a way that was both functional and inviting. The reception area and the restaurant were strikingly attractive. This had to do with more than bright colours and the smell of coffee. The staff and volunteers went about their work with a friendliness and warmth that, judging by the uptake, seemed to hit the right note with local people.

Section 4 *Case Studies of Five Faith-based Organisations*

This was a group of people who had taken up a considered position. They had made links on their own terms with the established Christian denominations, rejecting any identification with the labels 'Catholic' or 'Protestant', and had opted for a fresh start with the New Church movement. The record of development outlined above illustrates how they showed themselves willing to take risks. They were seen to be willing to make, and to learn from, mistakes. Their tenacity was plain. For more than a decade their respect for and confidence in the potential of the local community were demonstrated and brought positive response. They believed their faith required them to see other individuals as human beings rather than categories. Their lack of institutional freight allowed a less encumbered approach to the question of what churches exist to do.

This basic question underpinned each stage of their progress to the Family Centre. It pressed itself upon the congregation back in 1990 and they took time together to lay out the nature and scope of the mission as they understood it. They identified three broad strands at that time - evangelism, reconciliation and social action. Within the third strand they singled out jobs and families for attention, both of which they believed to be areas of difficulty and pressure for local people. They invited one of their members with a background in overseas aid and development to facilitate the interest group on the social action strand. He was now the centre manager. The team that emerged around him represented an impressive concentration of energy, creativity and commitment.

Cliff believed that he had genuine support from the CFC congregation. He recognised that a gap can open up between activists and congregation, but the church elders were aware of the danger. They worked to keep everyone in the picture. A prayer support group, made up of members of the congregation, took time to reflect on all aspects of the centre and to follow through in a practical capacity. 'It is seen as God's project, not a community minded splinter group', said one. The church members were encouraged to own the work, to make use of the facilities on offer, to get involved in a volunteer capacity. When 'the wee house' got going, church cell groups joined in with the pre-renovation work. The connection between congregation and activists, between reflection and action, was implicit in Cliff's words.

> *It's working. We're bursting at the seams at present, so it is a time to take stock again. We're not here just to keep doing the same thing. But we're not here to do things just because they're possible either. We have to know why we're doing it and it has to be within the areas we have identified as important - jobs and families.*

The best thing about Oasis was pinpointed as 'seeing hope in people's lives'. This came from a staff member who knew unemployment from the inside, the accompanying loss of a sense of self, the times when he felt himself to be 'treated as a nobody'. 'At Oasis people are treated as people. It's just natural', he said. He went on to describe how when the natural dignity of people is respected they begin to see themselves in a new light.

> *It even surprises them. And this enthuses and encourages us. Sometimes they ask questions about faith.*

The underpinning faith is crystallized in a verse from the New Testament displayed on an office wall. It is 1 John 3, v. 18, which reads 'let us love, not in word or speech, but in truth and action'. This is the mandate they took for their project, calling it 'love-in-action'. When the team worked to develop a theological rationale for what they were doing they boiled down what was important to some points on a single sheet of paper. They gained an understanding of their programme as a channel for outcomes wider than the ones they intended. They expressed it this way.

> *We're not after success as such. People keep coming. It's not all down to us. We serve and we leave the rest to God. We're not into counting souls saved, though when someone asks about Christian faith as a result of seeing the way people are treated here we're delighted* (Respondent 2).

In an area that is 96 percent Protestant, it is debatable how far this 'love-in-action' can reach out to bridge entrenched positions, especially when tensions rise. The year 2001 was a difficult one. From early May a pattern of frequent rioting close by the centre began. An Australian tourist was murdered in the area. A fence had to be erected around a street at the interface. Oasis representatives joined in weekly talks between members of local churches and two Protestant paramilitary groups. Two youth clubs, usually closed in the summer, were opened until 4am nightly 'for kids otherwise on the loose'. Programmes continued at Oasis, but

> *two people locked up rather than one. We want to build bridges, but we need to be careful. It's OK to go away somewhere, but within the local scene it can be dangerous. We are into a long process of trust building. It moves very slowly* (Respondent 2).

Section 4 Case Studies of Five Faith-based Organisations   89

Trust building appeared to be moving and growing steadily amongst community workers in the area. Significant contact across the divide created real and shared expertise in the development of joint projects. One of these involved Oasis in work with the community association from a local Catholic enclave to train people in basic IT skills (up to NVQ level 2) to equip them to staff a call centre established in the area. Work placements were deliberately mixed to include Protestant and Catholic people. Oasis took the lead role in this cooperative project because at the time it had funding capacity that the other organisation did not have.

Cooperation like this may be seen as an outworking of the CFC congregation's inclusive philosophy. It reflects the serious cross-community networking that goes on in the church itself. The church is organised on the cell model and the local cells have their own way of bedding in within their local area. At the time of this study there was a Sunday night forum once each month when the congregation hosted a meeting at which an invited speaker made a presentation and engaged in dialogue with the audience. Parties from across the whole political spectrum have been drawn in to these events, as have representatives from other groups like the Garvaghy Road residents from Portadown. The programme, like the creative arts work with young people, set out unapologetically to increase understanding, to open minds and to turn people into 'agents of change'. The faith development course too was open to people of any religious background and worship along with members of a Catholic church was taking place regularly.

This project built up a bank of statistics on numbers of people in training, numbers trained and in work. The training rooms were well equipped and perceived by one participant as unthreatening. Unemployed people were addressed individually and issues of confidence building, job search and interview skills looked at with care. Each person's training and re-training options were discussed and advice and support offered on a personal basis.

'Preparation for employment' is one module of an education programme written specially for the Oasis project and accredited by the Open College Network. Another is 'Bridging the learning gap' through which some women take a step into life-long learning. Another course enables parents to read successfully with their children and to choose material suited to their needs.

The team at Oasis know that work of this kind is difficult to measure. It is about confidence building, changing thought patterns, nurturing hope. They find great difficulty in making it real for potential funding bodies whose project based approach requires specific outcomes. Oasis was 'too busy at first for us to keep detailed records of what difference was being made', but they started what they called a 'credibility file'. It estimates medium to high local ownership. (95 percent of their activists were local people). Cliff feels that Oasis has reached a point where they are perceived as well earthed in the locality. Judging by the comments on the drop-in area for children, the quality and turnover of stock in the re-tog shop, the numbers in the restaurant on each field visit, Oasis has established a reputation for friendliness, enthusiasm and high standards.

Section 4 Case Studies of Five Faith-based Organisations   91

CASE 5: MORNINGTON COMMUNITY PROJECT, BELFAST

Inside, the café belies its inconspicuous frontage on the unpromising street by turning out to be warm and welcoming. Hardly a table is vacant. Everyone seems to know everyone else. The buzz of conversation never falters as, bearing my mug of tea and biscuit, I make my way to the service area and then to one of the few available seats. People come and go in a relaxed and familiar manner. Staff perform their duties with ease and obvious spirit. This is Mornington's community café, a combination of drop-in, advice centre, meeting place, news service, all purpose resource and safe space for the people of the locality.

In a quieter room above the café Ken, the Mornington director, spoke of the genesis of the project in 1989 and of how it emerged out of an initiative by local people who were impelled to respond to the needs of the unemployed young folk in the neighbourhood at that time. They opened a youth club with a modest unemployment programme and eventually procured appropriate premises in the area as well as the funding to set up a full time post. Ken felt that this sense of local roots had never been lost in the years since, nor had the growth of the organisation tempted it into reaching beyond its capacity. He knew about this. He was the first director. Monica, the project manager, had also been in post and part of the process since the early days. They share a firm sense of the strength that comes from embeddedness in the community and the advantages flowing from remaining manageable in size.

Initially there was no deliberate intention to set up a faith-based organisation. The originators did not as a group come from, or identify with, any church. When they appointed Ken as director, he relocated to the area with his family. He began to get to know the neighbourhood, walking around the streets, engaging in conversations with people on their doorsteps and in the shops. As part of the process he made contact with the local churches. One of them in particular seemed like it might be a potential source of volunteers. He actively sought out people from that congregation to discuss his ideas for Mornington. To some of them this came as a challenge and they were invited to commit a year of their time to the project. They did not ask their church, or indeed any other church, to endorse their work or to take responsibility for any aspect of the Mornington project.

However, as word of the project spread on the churches' informal networks across the city, people from a range of religious backgrounds began to show an interest. In some cases this turned into a serious voluntary commitment of time. Ken and his colleagues found themselves engaging with local people in a quality of relationship that spilled over into an attachment to the patch and that brought a sense of personal growth to the volunteers. In some the attachment became so strong that they gave up their existing church membership. Ken thought that some churches began to view Mornington with suspicion at that point. Yet it did not see or present itself as a faith-based organisation.

In setting up training and work experience activities Mornington developed a policy of being of use to the weakest. The activities were governed by the needs of the people who came to the centre and by the limited local job prospects. Many of the young unemployed people who were attracted to the centre had already been rejected by other training agencies. They showed they had very low numeracy and literacy skills. A survey of local employment possibilities revealed openings in community care, in clerical work and in retail and catering businesses. Consequently the centre offered opportunities for cashier work that would build skills in label reading and in basic arithmetic. By such unspectacular means, a quite dramatic change was brought about in the lives of many individuals.

Joe is one example. An isolated young man who had never been employed, he had no expectation of finding work, having been through the books of several training agencies. With little self-esteem or personal dignity, he was given a job and provided with support in the community café. There, with people who had an interest in him always at hand, his bearing and behaviour changed in response to the sense of acceptance he found. The community's understanding of him changed too and his own family members reported a wholly new side to him.

These qualities of acceptance, support and care that were promoted through training and fostered amongst staff and customers alike in the café environment also characterised other activities on the project. They could be seen in the work of Caroline, a board member from the beginning of the project and a teacher by profession. She concentrated on 'the kids who don't get to be in the school play', in order to help them expand their horizons. The qualities were a feature of the relationships between volunteers and young people in the youth group. Indeed some of the volunteers were designated as 'carers'. These leaders entered into a close year-long relationship with two young people. In this time they undertook to work together to enhance the social, vocational and spiritual development of the youngsters. A young Canadian husband and wife who were on placement spoke

Section 4 Case Studies of Five Faith-based Organisations   93

of it as a mutually rewarding experience and they reported the ending of their year on the project as 'like a bereavement experience'.

These qualities of support and care that were built into Mornington's programmes are also valued across the whole community. After particularly dreadful shootings at a nearby pub local residents naturally converged on the café, knowing they could find out about what had happened, feeling it to be a safe space where they could together give voice to their fear and anger. It has continued to represent a sense of security for them since that time.

By such patient and painstaking means and through such significant events the staff and volunteers at Mornington carved out their place in the neighbourhood. Project workers became familiar figures in the community and were quite often presented with concerns by people in the street. 'It takes me an hour and a half to buy a pint of milk at the top of our street' (Respondent 1). This simple comment says much about the ease with which people brought their concerns to the organisation. This ease was reflected in returns from evaluation exercises where reference was repeatedly made to a sense of family in the project. It was described in terms of something going beyond organisational links. Its effect was to enable people who would not necessarily do so to engage with each other across classes and age ranges. It was reflected in the high level of regard for the director and his wife in the locality and the appreciation of the open door policy that the project operated. These methods and their impact on the lives of so many people of all ages earned the respect of the local community and won its trust. They did not however bring stability to the project in terms of immunity from the vicissitudes of funding policy.

Two periods of crisis in the life of this organisation can each be related to the fragility of funding. When the ACE scheme was phased out, government provision in Northern Ireland shifted from support of groups working for reconciliation to single community group work. This was perceived to be an exercise to build on the ceasefires and buy people into the peace process. Some community organisations, previously blacklisted because of paramilitary links, now found themselves eligible for funding. But the policy change hit Mornington hard, denying it some 60 percent of the funding which had sustained its programmes for the first five years of its existence. Suddenly they felt 'a bit like a bunch of people with no real reason to continue'. Yet they could not gainsay or walk away from what had been achieved. They put it to themselves like this.

> *If we should continue, let's work out why. Then we can work out how we can go on* (Respondent 1).

Some hard thinking resulted in a new mission statement, one that for the first time was open about what had been until then their tacit basis in Christian faith. Coming out in this way might have presented something of a risk, but this was 1996. By then they had an established presence in the community, they knew they had proved themselves and were trusted. Besides they felt they had to respond to a challenge from a local observer who told them that he saw them as a Christian group who needed to be honest about their work. Thus they found a renewed sense of direction and purpose. They began to find they could tap into other sources of goodwill and support.

> *We've named what has existed for years. We have the ease of knowing what we're about. We're relaxed, open and confident about faith. People have responded to that* (Respondent 1).

The internal dialogue, ongoing since volunteers from different church backgrounds had come together in the early nineties to form a community of interest in the work, now focused on how to be a Christian project. The director lived with the ambiguities and mediated between those who saw the task in terms of evangelism and those who wanted to prioritise social need. Along with this internal dialogue there was continuing dialogue with the people of the neighbourhood, virtually inevitable since most of the staff were local. In addition, few of the 200 or so people on the various programmes were slow to express an opinion on anything. Out of this shared debate came an idea for a faith development module to be part of the programme. Started in 1998, it sat naturally alongside the sustained attempt to promote understanding between Catholic and Protestant people that permeated all of this FBO's activities. Like the cross-community work that flowed from this, it was natural and not contrived. Discussion of common everyday issues of a social, economic or political nature led into questions of faith.

Faith as an empowering factor played a part in a period of particular financial difficulty. At a point when they had no means of paying staff to run the full complement of programmes, volunteers kept them going on the basis that it was simply unacceptable to shut them down, that they should go on in hope.

> *It relates to faith. There's something in the air here, very hard to define, but it is very real, whole and evident; something spiritual that is sustaining and promoting the work* (Respondent 3).

Section 4 Case Studies of Five Faith-based Organisations   95

A task force emerged from within the local community. In late 2001 and into 2002 it produced some new publicity material which included an invitation to become a stakeholder. The new literature referred in its first paragraph to the community projects, set them in the light of the 'values of the Kingdom of God' and reported that 250 people use the project every week. It provided a confident and unembroidered outline of a plan to guarantee Mornington's core funding and an invitation to be part of that plan. Another leaflet spoke of Mornington's 'privilege and pain to work for social justice and reconciliation in this community of contrasting characters and experiences'. It illustrated more fully the extent of the work going on, then plainly spoke of the 'narrowing of the channels by which public moneys are distributed to the Community Sector' and of the need to establish an independent funding support network.

Here was Mornington celebrating a renewed sense of itself and projecting an image not of a group of outsiders there working for the people, or even with the people, but of the people themselves in that place flexing their participatory muscles through the medium of this FBO. In this it has crossed a line beyond the service provider role or the project initiating function into a measure of community leadership.

SECTION 5   *THE SURVEY*

The section lays out information produced by the 88 returns from the survey, examines the main findings and presents some characteristics of the people who are engaged in the work of the organisations profiled in the study.

SURVEY PURPOSE, DISTRIBUTION AND RESPONSE RATE

The purpose of the survey was to produce data and analysis that would increase understanding of the relationships between churches and their respective communities in Northern Ireland.

Appendices I and II provide the rationale for using questions on social capital from the Onyx and Bullen study of 1997. The survey questionnaire, published in full in Appendix IV, was distributed through the leadership of each organisation. On the occasion of the first interview with the minister or leader, ten questionnaires were given over for handing on to members for self-administration along with stamped addressed envelopes for return. This provided opportunity for the researcher to outline the need for respondents to present a balanced picture of the organisation by age, gender, status and length of membership.

When it is recalled that the organisations were selected for the promise of their work, to represent different geographic areas of the country and to include a range of religious denominations, it will be obvious that they do not offer a unified set of entities for study or comparison and are not intended to reflect an equal balance of Catholic and Protestant organisations or people. Hence the data may be indicative of patterns and trends, but they do not support definite comparisons based upon religious difference.

Of the 120 questionnaires distributed 88 were returned, a response rate of 73 percent. A breakdown of returns by FBO is given over.

Section 5 *The Survey*

Table 3: Questionnaire returns by organisation

	FBO Name	FBO Location	Questionnaires returned
1	Flax	Belfast	4
2	Holy Family	Belfast	5
3	Omagh Boys & Girls Club	Omagh	10
4	Ballysillan	Belfast	8
5	'Benmoe'	'Ballycarn'	8
6	Knocknagoney	Belfast	8
7	Shankill	Lurgan	6
8	City Mission	Londonderry	9
9	Barnabas	Enniskillen	6
10	YMCA (Central)	Belfast	7
11	Oasis	Belfast	9
12	Mornington	Belfast	8
			Total 88

SURVEY ANALYSIS

Information from the questionnaires was fed into a computer package for analysing quantitative data (SPSS for Windows) to produce a profile of the sample. Analysis proceeded by way of interrogation of the answers to questions clustered around the following themes:

- the local community and respondents' relation to it
- reciprocity and local trust
- voluntary action, broader participation and civic engagement
- religious behaviour
- personal attitudes, values and beliefs
- people and networks
- social capital infrastructure.

These data were then examined for fit with the interview findings on cross-community benefit, community cohesion and social capital formation.

PROFILE OF THE SAMPLE
(This cluster includes questions 1-11. The full questionnaire appears in Appendix IV).

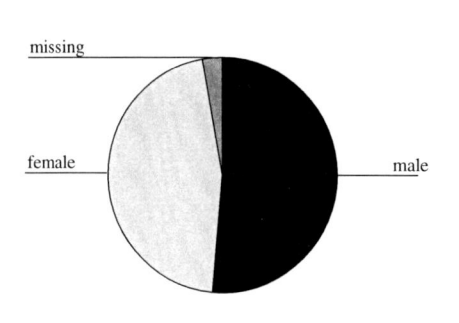

Pie Chart 1: Gender of respondents

Bar Chart 1: Marital status of respondents

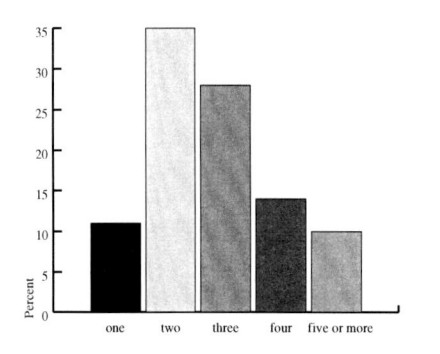

Bar Chart 2: Number of children

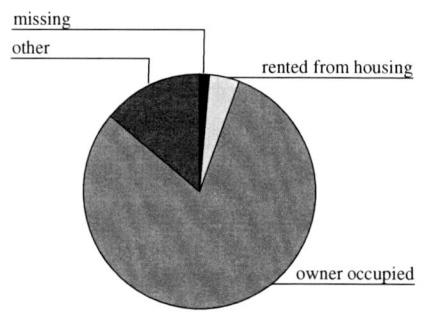

Pie Chart 2: Tenure of household

Section 5 The Survey 99

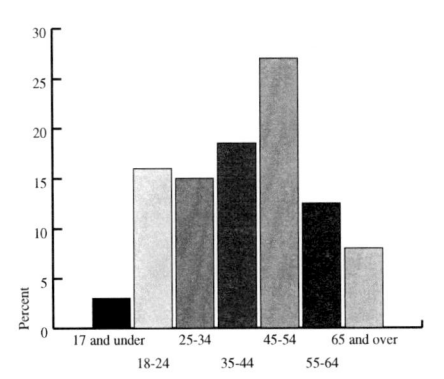

Bar Chart 3: Age category of respondents

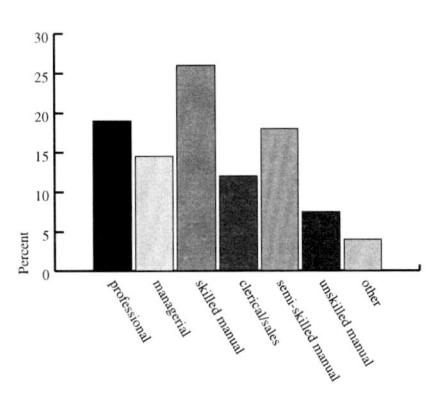

Bar Chart 4: Home background of upbringing

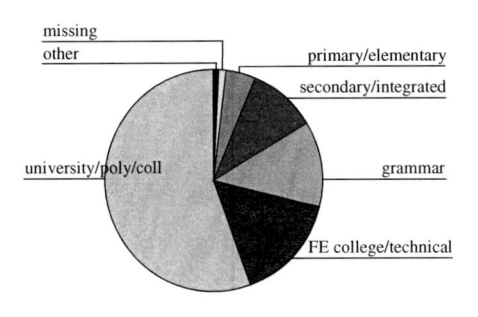

Pie Chart 3: Most recent full-time education background

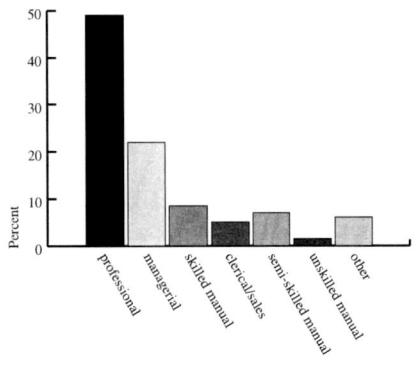

Bar Chart 5: Current home

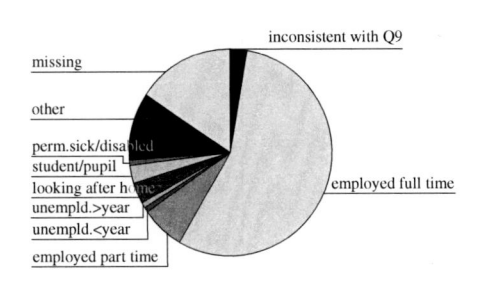

Pie Chart 4: Current employment status

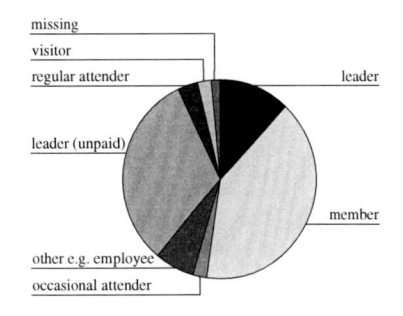

Pie Chart 5: Status in church/FBO

The survey respondents are evenly balanced by gender (Pie Chart 1). While just 3 percent of the respondents are aged 17 or under and 8 percent are 65 or over, most are in the 45-54 age range followed by the 35-44 range (Bar Chart 3). Two thirds are married, most with two or more children (Bar Charts 1 & 2). A small percentage is widowed or divorced, but most of the remaining third of the sample have never married (Bar Chart 1). Over three quarters own their homes (Pie Chart 2). Over half have experienced higher education (Pie Chart 3). Whereas 18 percent were born into a professional home background, 45 percent now describe their present home background as professional (Bar Charts 4 & 5). Full time employment engages 54 percent, part time 7 percent. Some 14 percent are retired and 1 percent have been unemployed for more than a year (Pie Chart 4). The sample includes 11 percent describing themselves as leaders, 6 percent as employees, 32 percent as in unpaid leadership positions and 41 percent as members of their churches/FBOs (Pie Chart 5). On the face of it this is a picture of a predominantly middle aged, middle class, comfortable and mainly Protestant (Bar Chart 6) group of family people who are mostly members of or voluntary leaders within the organisations that feature in this study.

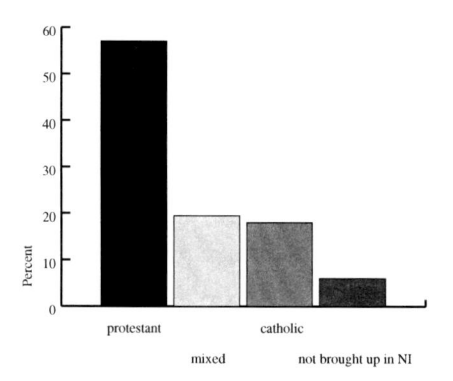

Bar Chart 6: *Religious background of respondents*

THE LOCAL COMMUNITY AND RESPONDENTS' RELATION TO IT
(This cluster includes questions 35-41, 16, 20b, 22, 26k, 42-61, 71, 72).

Respondents were not asked to give their religious denomination. Question 35 (see Bar Chart 6 above) is framed to enquire into the neighbourhood in which each

Section 5 The Survey 101

was brought up (Were you brought up in a Protestant, Catholic or mixed area of Northern Ireland?). It is important to remember two things at this point. The first is that the response to the question does not necessarily indicate the religious affiliation of the individual. The second is that several of the management committees and boards of the FBOs in the study are religiously mixed. Therefore it should be assumed neither that the 19 responses from Catholic based organisations all come from Catholic respondents nor that the other 69 all come from Protestants. The figures show that, of the respondents brought up in Northern Ireland (all but 6 percent), 56 percent come from a mostly Protestant and 19 percent from a predominantly Catholic area. The remainder grew up in a mixed area. 18 percent report that they now live in single community areas and 26 percent say that they live in areas with about equal numbers. For 61 percent of the sample, the area has stayed about the same over the last five years (Pie Charts 6 & 7).

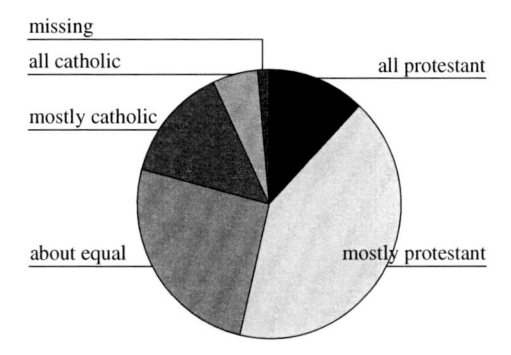

Pie Chart 6: Perceptions of current religious makeup of neighbourhood

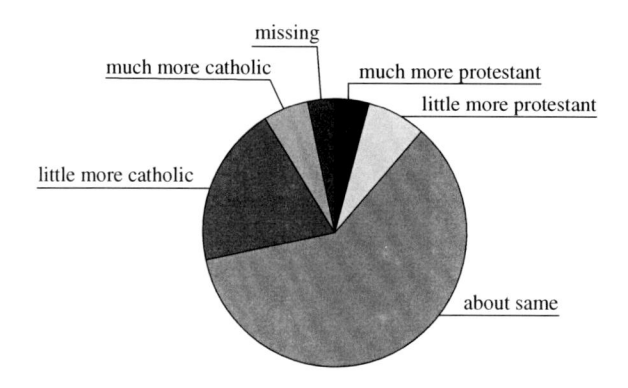

Pie Chart 7: Perceptions of change to religious makeup of neighbourhood

The people in the sample are not insulated from the random violence that accompanies life in Northern Ireland. Four respondents had moved house because of intimidation and six reported experience of bomb damage to their homes. Some 26 respondents have known a neighbour injured or killed, 18 a close friend. The 20 who indicated that a relative had known serious injury or death in the Troubles came from across the range of organisations in the study (Table 4).

Table 4: Number of respondents with relative seriously injured or killed in the Troubles

FBO Affiliation	
Catholic	7
Presbyterian	1
Church of Ireland	3
Methodist	4
New Church	2
Unaffiliated	3

Three quarters of the respondents attend worship in their local area, the bulk of them reporting their church as 'like a family', one to which they have a strong sense of belonging. Though more are satisfied than unsatisfied, 35 percent of the

Section 5 The Survey 103

sample think that their church could be doing more to educate members about local area problems and social issues. Some 70 percent have attended a local community event in the past six months (Pie Chart 8) and about 60 percent are active members in other local organisations or clubs (Pie Chart 9). In addition, 53 percent are on the committee of other local organisations. A quarter of the respondents have been involved in dealing with a local emergency and 59 percent in a local community project over the past five years.

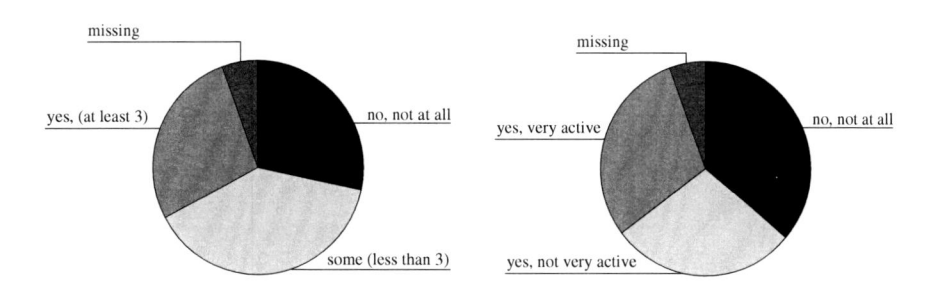

Pie Chart 8: *Attendance at recent local community event*   **Pie Chart 9**: *Active membership of local organisation*

Most people feel at home in their local area (Pie Chart 16) and for half of the sample this is definitely the case.

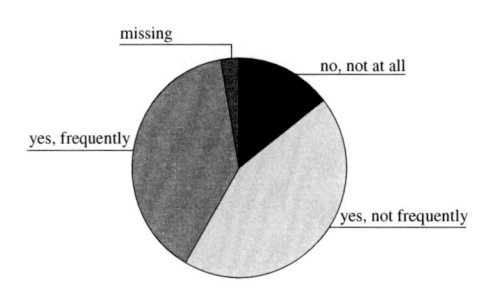

Pie Chart 10: *Percentage of respondents reporting that they have picked up rubbish recently*

About 85 percent care enough about their locality to pick up rubbish in a public place (Pie Chart 10). Although 38 percent say they feel very safe walking in the neighbourhood after dark, 58 percent consider themselves safe, but not very safe. A third of the respondents think that their area has a reputation for being a safe place.

Over 70 percent feel that most people can be trusted, but not very much (Pie Chart 15). About 50 percent say they would definitely be willing to provide access to a telephone in their home if someone's car broke down nearby. Most people are confident about sources of information if they need help with a life decision, free enough to express a minority viewpoint and willing to seek mediation in any dispute with a neighbour. Two thirds of the sample have visited a neighbour in the past week (Bar Chart 8) and 57 percent are sure they could get help from a neighbour when they need it, but this drops to 43 percent who are sure about leaving a child in a neighbour's care (Bar Chart 9). Around 60 percent say they nearly always run into friends or acquaintances when shopping in the local area. While 36 percent of the sample are themselves definitely open to the idea of living among people of different lifestyles (Pie Chart 11), 27 percent think that their neighbours would definitely accept a stranger moving into the street, with 64 percent not totally sure about this (Pie Chart 12).

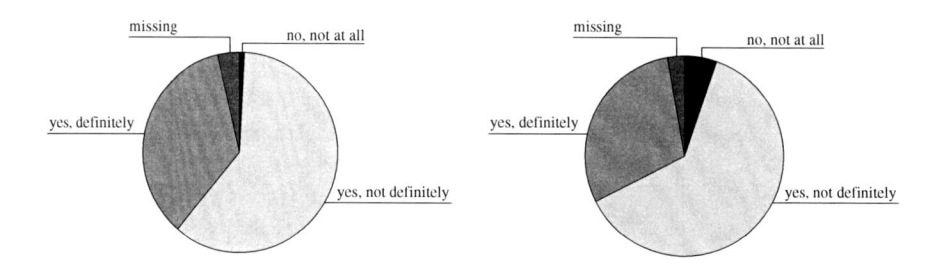

Pie Chart 11: *Respondents reporting that they are open to living amongst people of different lifestyles*

Pie Chart 12: *Respondents reporting whether a stranger moving into the street would be accepted*

Section 5 The Survey

RECIPROCITY AND LOCAL TRUST
(This cluster includes questions 18d, g-l, 26l, 38, 46, 47, 51, 54, 55, 57-60, 64, 79).

Almost three quarters of the sample say they have tried to build a friendship across the religious divide and roughly the same proportion say that they have helped someone out with food, clothing or money more than once (Pie Charts 13 & 14).

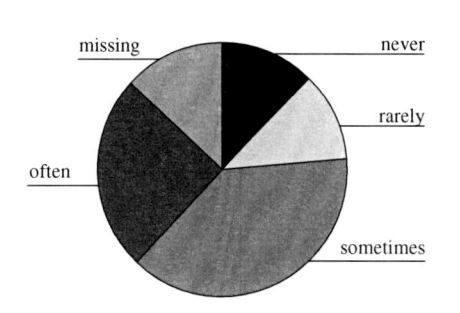

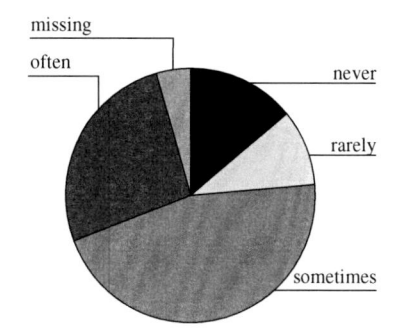

Pie Chart 13: *Respondents reporting that they have tried to make friendships across the religious divide*

Pie Chart 14: *Respondents reporting that they had provided someone in need with food, clothes or money*

About 45 percent of the respondents have been of help to someone who was searching for a job and around half of the sample sometimes or often provide informal care for sick or handicapped people. Over half sometimes or often volunteer transport or childcare and most people have offered personal comfort or support to someone more than once, with 11 percent having provided emergency housing.

Encouraging people to look out for (minister to) others in these ways in their daily lives is an aspect of church life that 78 percent find somewhat or very satisfactory. This, along with 74 percent reporting that they prefer to live in a neighbourhood with an equal balance of Catholic and Protestant neighbours (Bar Chart 7), is indicative of some readiness for give and take on the part of people in the sample.

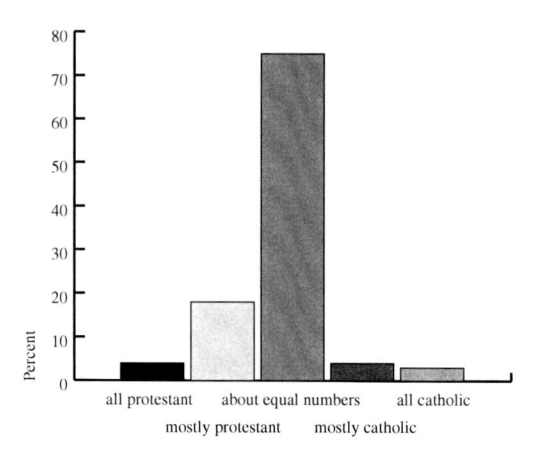

Bar Chart 7: Response to the question of neighbourhood preference (Q. 38)

An expressed willingness by 25 percent to join local community action in the face of emergency may be another indicator of this tendency towards solidarity. The participation in a local community project by around 60 percent may also signal this disposition towards others. Most people feel themselves free to speak out in disagreement with what others are agreed upon, but well over half of the sample, 56 percent, have reservations about doing so.

The same pattern appears in response to the question on trusting most people, where the overwhelming majority are positive, but over 70 percent express caution (Pie Chart 15). Similarly, when asked if they would offer help to someone whose car had broken down outside their house, around 45 percent lean towards offering access to a home telephone, but not with certainty. Almost the same percentage of the sample are less than definite about feeling at home in their local neighbourhood (Pie Chart 16).

Section 5 The Survey

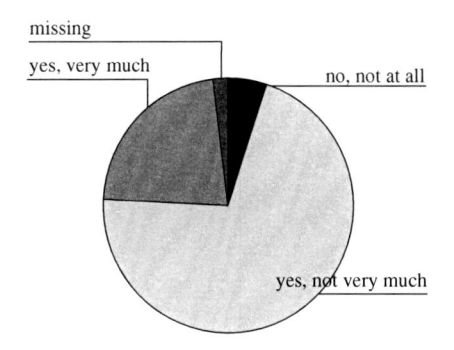

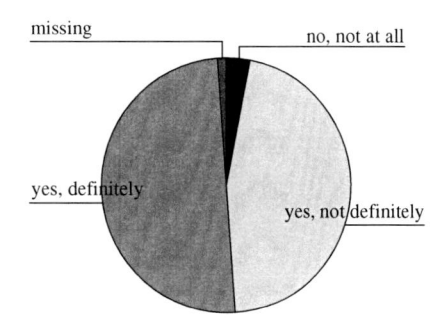

Pie Chart 15: *Respondents' feeling about trusting most people*

Pie Chart 16: *Respondents and feeling at home in locality*

The figure showing people who are not sure of getting help from neighbours, 40 percent, is close to that indicating uncertainty about asking a neighbour to look after a child, 36 percent (Bar Chart 9). Two thirds had visited a neighbour in the past week but, for 40 percent, such an activity is not frequent. A shared meal at the weekend with people outside the household is something that over 70 percent enjoy, yet for 42 percent it is not frequent, and for 30 percent it is not usual. One third of the sample are very hopeful about the possibility of building enough trust for a stable future for Northern Ireland. Most people are cautious in their hope.

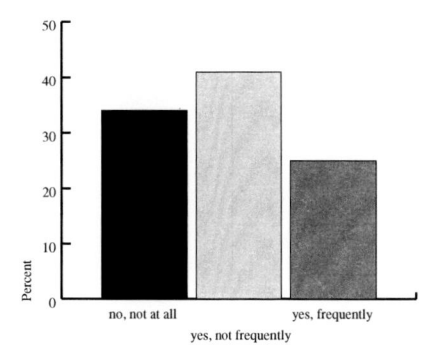

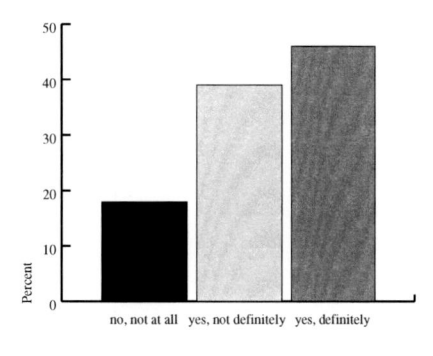

Bar Chart 8: *Visits to neighbours in past week*

Bar Chart 9: *Readiness to ask neighbour to care for child*

VOLUNTARY ACTION, BROADER PARTICIPATION AND CIVIC ENGAGEMENT
(This cluster includes 13g-i, 17, 23d, 26a,b,d,j,k, 31d,g, 34b, 42-48, 74, 75).

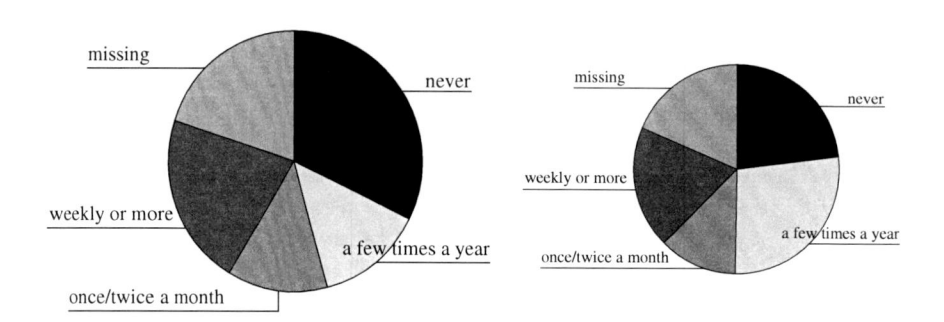

Pie Chart 17: *Respondents' participation in community organising/development work*

Pie Chart 19: *Respondents' participation in voluntary work outside church/FBO*

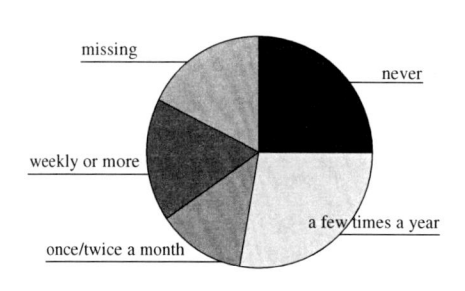

Pie Chart 18: *Respondents' participation in other civic and community groups*

As shown here, in addition to involvement within their own faith-based organisations, around half of the sample participate in some kind of community development work (Pie Chart 17), in other civic and community groups (Pie Chart 18), or in voluntary work beyond the church (Pie Chart 19). Of those so engaged, 13 are leaders and 45 are on the management committee of another local group.

Training sponsored by FBOs in reconciliation or cross-community work had been taken up by 20 percent of the respondents, lay leadership by 17 percent and community or economic development ministries by 12 percent.

Section 5 The Survey   109

Addressing social justice issues and working towards political change is reckoned to be most important for church/FBO leaders to do by 39 percent of the sample. Three spheres of engagement with the community, namely social service, neighbourhood development and assisting young people with values and life skills, are considered to be satisfactory in their organisations by 66 percent, 79 percent and 71 percent respectively.

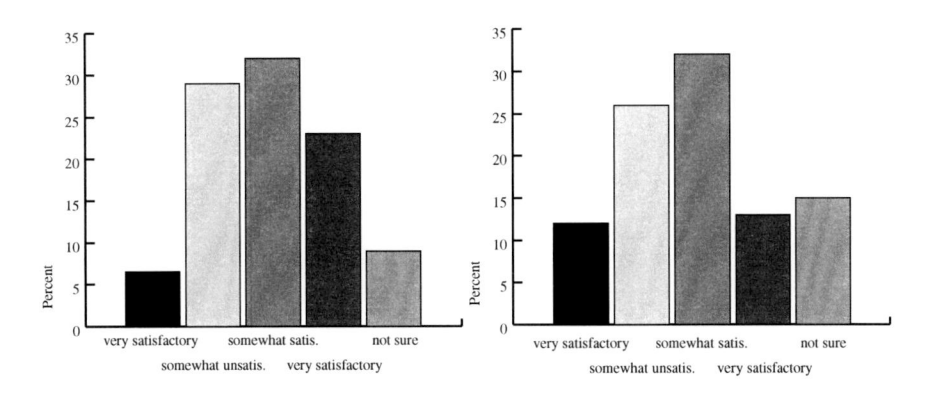

Bar Chart 10: Respondents' perceptions of their organisation's work to educate the church on local area problems

Bar Chart 11: Respondents' perceptions of their organisation's work to organise groups to change society or influence politics

Some 56 percent think that the work of their organisation to educate the church on local area problems and social issues is satisfactory (Bar Chart 10). Fewer (45 percent) think that their church or faith-based organisation is working satisfactorily to change society or influence politics (Bar Chart 11). It would require further analysis to ascertain whether these perceptions reflect a desire for more or less of these activities.

79 percent of the respondents agree that "our actions can create a much better society than now exists", 57 percent agree that poverty is largely due to social, economic and political factors and 65 percent rate an active search for social and economic justice "very important" or "essential". Help to a local group other than church is being offered at least once a week by 23 percent and, of the 60 percent involved in another local organisation, half are very active. Just over 50 percent say they are committee members (Pie Chart 20).

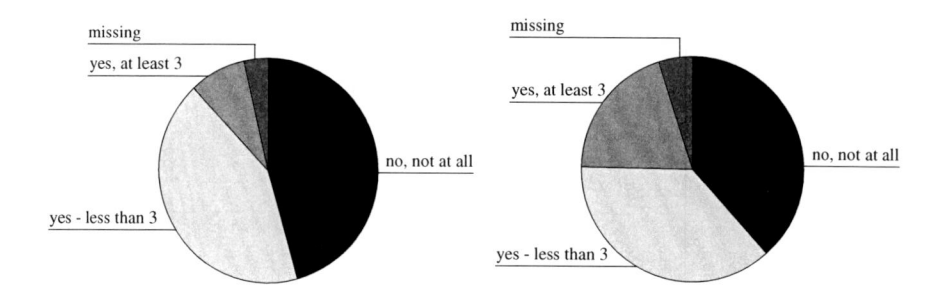

Pie Chart 20: Respondents' membership on other local management committee

Pie Chart 21: Respondents' involvement in local community project

In the past five year period, a local community project involved 57 percent of the sample (Pie Chart 21) and 24 percent had been part of a local community action to deal with an emergency. At one time or another 53 percent had engaged in a project to organise a new service in the area; 70 percent had attended a recent local community event.

In all this activity, under half of the respondents feel they have a great deal of control over their lives and a quarter feel that they are valued very much by society. On the other hand, 5 percent feel that they are not much valued.

RELIGIOUS BEHAVIOUR
(This cluster includes questions 11, 12, 13a-e, 15, 16, 17, 18, 28).

Of the sample, 41 percent describe themselves as members of their organisation, 32 percent as unpaid leaders and 11 percent as leaders. Employees and attenders make up 13 percent. Most respondents became involved in their church/FBO through family membership (Pie Chart 22), the exceptions being some parachurches, where returns come from people on placement or in employment at the project and from people whose involvement has been triggered through a friendship. For 82 percent of the sample participation in worship is weekly or

Section 5 The Survey   111

more often (Pie Chart 24). For 76 percent the place of worship is in the local neighbourhood (Pie Chart 23), while 21 percent travel outside.

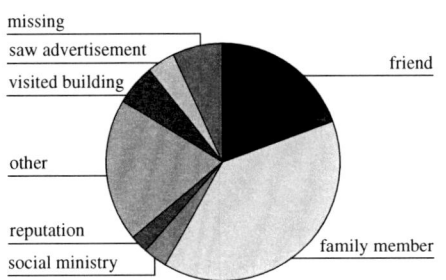

Pie Chart 22: How respondents became involved with their church/FBO

Pie Chart 23: Respondents' location of acts of worship

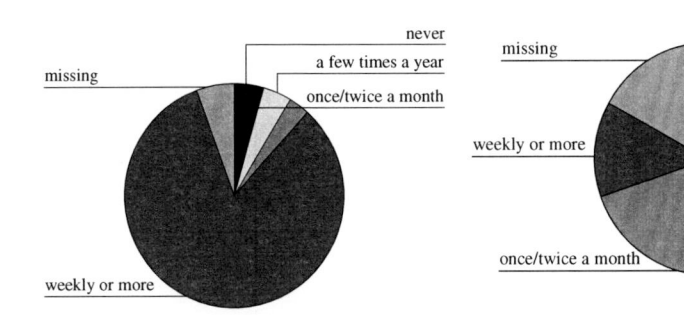

Pie Chart 24: Respondents' participation in acts of worship

Pie Chart 25: Respondents' participation in church FBO committees

The study of scripture is at least a weekly activity for 26 percent of the sample. A quarter these people are involved in teaching groups or in Sunday school and almost half are in work with young people that engages them weekly or more often. Frequent meetings with the leader or minister of their FBO happen for 27 percent and more than a monthly committee or board meeting also involves 41 percent.

Sponsored training in lay leadership was taken up by 17 percent and in evangelism by 11 percent. The level of involvement in their organisation has increased over the last few years for well over half the sample.

About 68 percent of the respondents speak about religious beliefs sometimes or often. It is rarely or never done by 32 percent. Roughly 31 percent have given religious literature away sometimes or often and 69 percent rarely or never. Bringing someone to church for the first time is unusual (85 percent rarely or never), but 73 percent have sometimes or often tried to make friends with a person of a different faith. This is rarely to study scripture (70 percent) or to lead someone to faith (76 percent). Provision of emergency housing has seldom been made (74 percent never) or help given to find a job (41 percent never), but food, clothing or money have been provided sometimes or often (75 percent), sick and handicapped cared for sometimes or often (50 percent), transport and/or childcare volunteered sometimes or often (52 percent). Comfort, counsel and prayer support have also been made available (76 percent sometimes or often).

These are people who are serious, if modest, about their faith. Over half of them believe their organisation gives as much attention to people outside the church as to those who are members and regular attenders. They are themselves ready to extend to others in need the kind of practical help and support that are within their reach without attempting to evangelise. As active members of their church or FBO they are willing to put time into its committees and boards. In addition members are to be found in leadership positions most often in work with young people and teaching groups and Sunday schools, followed by leadership on committees and boards.

PERSONAL ATTITUDES, VALUES AND BELIEFS
(This cluster includes questions 19, 20, 22, 23, 26, 31, 32, 34, 38, 42, 51, 54, 70, 71, 73-80).

Question 19 asks about the reasons why respondents engage in voluntary activities within their organisations. Few are interested in adding to church membership or doing what their leaders expect. Most are concerned to show compassion to people in need (76 percent of the sample). Next comes experiencing God in a deeper way at 46 percent. Third is showing thanks for what God has done at 44 percent. Fourth equal at 42 percent comes helping to make society more just and obeying a sense of call or direction from God. A difference emerges in the order that these motivations are rated by respondents from Catholic based or Protestant based organisations and it is shown in the table below.

Table 5: Question 19. The top four responses rated extremely important

Joint response	Catholic based FBO	Protestant based FBO
Showing compassion	Showing compassion	Showing compassion
Deeper experience of God	Making society more just	Deeper experience of God
Giving thanks	Deeper experience of God and giving thanks	Giving thanks and obeying God's call
Making society more just and obeying God's call	Obeying God's call	Making society more just

Note. Oasis, not being a Catholic based FBO, is included here in the Protestant based FBO column.

At question 20, which invites respondents to choose from a list of words that might be used to describe a church, the two highest scoring descriptions together give a picture of church as a compassionate community partner. Question 22 enquires about the respondents' sense of belonging to their church or faith-based organisation and 94 percent report that it is strong.

Respondents considered the top two most important functions of church/FBO leadership (question 23) to be 'helping people grow spiritually' (81 percent) and 'applying scripture to modern day issues' (76 percent). The bottom two were 'coordinating social ministry programmes' (42 percent) and 'addressing social justice issues and working towards political change' (39 percent). Again there was a difference of emphasis amongst the organisations. It is interesting that, of the top scoring functions, 'helping people grow spiritually' was voted most important by 100 percent of the respondents from the Catholic parish, the Methodist faith-based organisation and the Presbyterian congregations. 'Applying scripture to modern day issues' was voted most important by 100 percent of the respondents from the Catholic parish and the two Presbyterian congregations. 'Addressing social justice and political change', perceived overall as the least important function of leadership, scored highest amongst New Church respondents (78 percent), followed by the Catholic parish (67 percent) and the unaffiliated faith-based organisation (60 percent). 12 percent of the respondents from the Presbyterian congregations and 8 percent from the Church of Ireland congregations saw it as most important.

At question 26, (How satisfactory do you think work is in the following areas of ministry activity in your church?) FBO activities given highest levels of satisfaction were assisting neighbourhood or community development (86 percent) and helping to deepen and guide the spiritual life of church attenders (84 percent). Then came providing aid and social services for people in need in the community (79 percent) followed by providing a caring ministry to people who are sick (79 percent). Lower satisfaction levels are shown towards organising groups to change society or influence politics (46 percent) and encouraging revivals and crusades (35 percent). Within the organisations, 78 percent of the respondents from the Methodist congregation and 67 percent of those from the Catholic parish thought their work in assisting community development was very satisfactory.

The question of interpretation remains. Level of satisfaction is not the same as level of approval or of level of activity. The fact that 5 percent of all respondents reported themselves very satisfied with their churches' efforts to organise revivals and crusades may mean that the majority want more of this activity. However, given the context provided by the case study material, it is likely that what is reflected in the responses to this question is indeed a degree of approval. Taking the example of the unaffiliated FBO, which is in fact a community development oriented project, 60 percent of the respondents from it said their work in this field was very satisfactory and none expressed satisfaction about encouraging revivals and crusades. On balance therefore, it would seem that the scores say something about the priorities of the FBOs in the study.

In responses to question 31a (For each set of statements listed below, please circle the number which best fits with your beliefs) most respondents (51 percent) agreed with both statements, namely that the task of the church is both to work to change society and to work to change the lives of individuals. However 36 percent emphasised changing individuals and 13 percent emphasised changing society.

A similar pattern of response continues throughout the seven sets of alternative statements presented in question 31. There was general agreement that the way to share God's love is both to talk and act, but 37 percent emphasised action, 8 percent talk. Most agreed that both government and church are responsible for meeting the needs of the poor, but 25 percent emphasised government, 7 percent the church. Most agreed that the church should focus both on life now and on a life to come, but 36 percent emphasised here and now, 5 percent looked beyond death. With 76 percent agreement that the church should care both for humanistic

Section 5 The Survey 115

wellbeing and relationships as well as spiritual wellbeing and relationships, 19 percent emphasised the spiritual and 5 percent the humanistic.

Two exceptions to the above pattern stand out. These are to do with beliefs about how to improve the condition of society (question 31d) and with the causes of poverty (question 31g). In the matter of improving society, there is a decisive swing to one end of the spectrum that scores higher than the central position of agreement with both. Some 79 percent agree that our actions can create a much better society than now exists. This is reflected across the denominational lines, ranging from 93 percent in Catholic respondents to 60 percent in the Methodist FBO.

In the matter of deciding whether poverty is caused more by foolish personal choices or by structural factors, 57 percent agreed that poverty is largely due to social, economic and political factors. But within the denominations, there were clear differences of opinion. In both the Methodist FBO and the unaffiliated FBO, 80 percent opted for social, economic and political factors, with the remaining 20 percent agreeing with both statements. The next highest score for structural factors came from the Catholic parish, with a 60 percent vote and 40 percent agreeing with both statements. In none of these three organisations was there a single vote for the case that poverty is due to personal choice. At the other end of the spectrum, two organisations returned scores that showed the majority of respondents within them agreeing with both statements. For example the Presbyterian congregations had 57 percent of their respondents agreeing that both personal and structural factors play a part in causing poverty, and 36 percent opting for structural factors.

In order to escape from poverty (question 32) 62 percent of the sample thought that people need a good education and a decent job. 54 percent thought they needed to be treated with dignity and respect. These were the two highest scoring factors. Lowest score went to better personal morals or lifestyle at 7 percent. A caring church family and a more just society, both at 37 percent, came ahead of adequate government support at 29 percent. The three top scoring essential qualities of a good life (question 34) were to maintain loving and stable family relationships (66 percent), to be a good citizen and community member (52 percent) and to practise religious values at home and at work (52 percent). While almost half of the sample saw the need to seek social and economic justice as very important, it came lowest among the essentials of the good life at 18 percent.

Over 70 percent of the respondents state a preference for living in a neighbourhood with about equal numbers of Catholic and Protestant residents, but a single community is also preferred by a minority on both sides. There is a willingness to work with people other than church members on the part of 53 percent of the sample and a definite readiness to express a minority point of view on the part of around 40 percent. Openness to others on the basis that they can be trusted very much is reported by 22 percent, but 6 percent say that most people are not at all to be trusted. Openness to others from a variety of different cultural or ethnic groups and lifestyles is claimed by 40 percent and 35 percent respectively. It is unwelcome to 4 percent and 1 percent respectively.

At question 73 (Which of the following groups of people would you prefer not to have as neighbours?) the categories are, in order of least welcome, people with a drug addiction (67 percent), people with extreme political views (62 percent) and heavy drinkers (59 percent). There is little objection to people of a different race (3 percent) or religion (1 percent).

Just under half of the sample feel they have a great deal freedom and control of life, while 52 percent believe they have some, but not a great deal. A quarter of the sample feel valued by society very much and 70 percent feel valued, but less than very much. Some 40 percent perceive themselves as very satisfied with their life as a whole and 59 percent as less than very satisfied.

Thoughts about the meaning and purpose of life come often to 51 percent of the sample, to 41 percent sometimes and to 8 percent rarely. A bright future for humanity is seen by 68 percent of the sample, a bleak one by 32 percent. As to hopes for a stable and peaceful future for Northern Ireland, these are mixed. One third are very hopeful, with 59 percent less than very hopeful and 8 percent not at all hopeful. Across all the organisations in the study there is more certainty about the need for churches to be more active in trying to improve relations between the communities in Northern Ireland, as Bar Chart 12 shows.

Section 5 The Survey

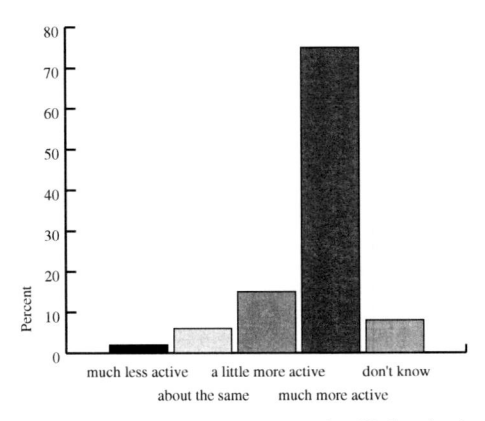

Bar Chart 12: *Responses to the question 'How active should churches be in trying to improve relations between the communities in Northern Ireland?'*

PEOPLE AND NETWORKS
(This cluster includes questions 3, 13, 17, 22, 34, 42-48, 58, 61-67).

Over half of the respondents (55 percent) are in families with two or more children. Those people whose children are of school age are brought immediately into contact with other parents, teachers and family service and support networks. All but 1 percent feel confident about getting help when necessary from the circle of neighbours whom they are likely to meet (59 percent) at local shops. Some 68 percent had spoken to more than ten people the previous day, over half had been in touch by telephone with more than six friends in the previous week and 70 percent had shared a weekend meal with people outside the household occasionally or regularly. All but 3 percent of those people in work feel themselves to be part of a team and 30 percent consider their colleagues to be part of their friendship as well as work networks.

Regular attendance at worship (for 82 percent weekly or more) places people within the network of their churches, for which 92 percent claim a strong sense of belonging. Involvement, for 54 percent an increasing involvement, in a range of church-related activities opens up contact with people and agencies beyond the church base. The 20 percent who have undertaken training in cross-community work will have been introduced to supportive networks within that field. 41 percent are members of church/FBO committees or boards and 35 percent participate in community development work. These people have opportunity to cooperate with others in partnerships and in shared initiatives. The community at whose wellbeing these efforts are aimed is one in which 85 percent of the respondents believe it important to be a good citizen. Pursuit of this includes, for 23 percent, help to a local group other than church at least once a week and 60 percent involvement in another local organisation, half as committee members. Linkages and networks, formal and informal, will have been strengthened through engagement in local community events and projects, in actions to deal with an emergency or to organise a new service in the area.

SOCIAL CAPITAL INFRASTRUCTURE
(This cluster includes questions 13d,g,i, 17, 20c,f,i, 26b,d,j,l, 46, 47, 48).

Almost half of the respondents said they are working with young people weekly or more often, 44 percent reported involvement in community development work of some kind and 36 percent are participating in other civic or community groups. A small percentage had taken advantage of training sponsored by their organisation in the sphere of community or economic development (12 percent) and cross-community work (20 percent). More than three quarters (76 percent) see their FBO as a community partner, 68 percent feel it is an empowering organisation and 73 percent believe it to be a social agent for change. Some 86 percent express satisfaction with their organisation's work to assist neighbourhood development and 46 percent are satisfied with attempts to organise groups that could have some influence on wider society and its politics. Helping young people to develop life skills and values and encouraging reciprocity are considered to be satisfactory aspects of the work of the organisations by 78 percent of the respondents.

Local action has engaged respondents in cooperative activity, whether to deal with an emergency (24 percent), to organise a new service for the area (53 percent) or to participate in a community project (57 percent).

There was a qualified yes to the notion that a cultural or ethnic mix might benefit a neighbourhood by 51 percent, with 40 percent giving it a definite 'yes' and 4 percent a definite 'no'. The idea of living among people of different lifestyles would be enjoyed 'definitely' by 35 percent, 'probably' by 60 percent and 'not at all' by 1 percent.

SUMMING UP

What is important for the project report is to isolate the survey findings that speak to the interview findings. Here it may be said that, on a broad reading, this is a group of people who have a strong sense of belonging to their church, yet over half of them are active in other local organisations. Two thirds of them rate an active search for social and economic justice as very important, even essential, for people of faith. They do not see the church as a branch of the social services, in fact they are quite clear about the need for church leadership to help people grow spiritually and to use the resources of their faith. But they are themselves more concerned to respond to people in need than to add to their church's membership. They want the church to be a compassionate community partner, to care for human well being and to assist neighbourhood development.

These are significant facts in the light of the well known theological distance between the churches and in view of the range of viewpoints within each organisation that is detectable in the survey data. Indeed the overall message from this research project should add weight to the argument of those who see inter-church and inter-faith discussion in Northern Ireland as potentially more purposeful and fruitful when based around the sharing of ideas and information on issues of public policy than when focused on matters of theology.

SECTION 6 *FINDINGS*

The section presents findings from the interviews and considers them under the headings:

- what churches and para-churches are doing;
- who benefits and how;
- cross-community benefit;
- community cohesion and social capital formation;
- leadership, funding and fragility.

Activities are categorised first by Broad Area:

- community support programmes;
- health programmes;
- social programmes;
- educational programmes;
- training programmes.

They are then categorised by Social Capital Domain:

- empowerment;
- participation;
- associational activity and common purpose;
- supporting networks and reciprocity;
- collective norms and values;
- trust;
- safety;
- belonging.

This section contains material from interviews with people engaged in the work of the churches and other faith-based organisations examined in the project. The material is organised around the three concepts identified for exploration in the original research proposal, namely 'cross-community benefit', 'community cohesion' and 'leadership'. In addition it lays out what churches and para-churches are doing by broad area and by social capital domain and points to beneficial outcomes. The chapter follows a logical structure with a presentation of

Section 6 Findings 121

the array of voluntary activities supported and an examination of who benefits from them and how they do so. It looks more closely at the interlinking cross-community, community cohesion and social capital dimensions to the activities of these bodies and then highlights the elements of leadership and funding as crucial for their sustainability and success.

THE INTERVIEWS

A total of 46 face-to-face interviews was conducted (3 for each of the 7 profiles and 5 for each of the 5 cases) with ministers, leaders, members of congregations, boards, committees and staff. They took place in the offices, workplaces or homes of the interviewees and were sometimes interrupted by the demands of their work or household. A schedule (see Appendix III) kept the interview on the track of necessary information and, in most cases, within time boundaries. However since some of the questions were deliberately open ended the one hour interview on occasions extended to twice that time. A tape recorder was not used. Notes were taken during the course of each interview and written up within twenty four hours.

WHAT CHURCHES AND PARA-CHURCHES ARE DOING

The interviews revealed that the twelve churches and para-churches that are the subject of this report are deeply engaged in voluntary activities that enable people to build a sense of growing as a community within areas of deprivation and social exclusion in Northern Ireland. Their voluntary activities are producing outcomes in line with those noted in the *Partners for Change* document of the Northern Ireland Department of Social Development (DSD, 2001). Those outcomes include:

- increased employability;
- greater attention to equality issues;
- the acquisition of new skills;
- increased community safety;
- a more supportive environment for children and young people;
- better community relations within and between communities;
- environmental improvement;
- developing community infrastructure in areas where it is weak.

The twelve organisations come from different strands of Christian faith and are located in different geographical settings. They are very different in character, in size, in durability, in how they define themselves and in the programmes they are operating. Yet in their differences they have qualities in common. Each shows signs of being aware of belonging to the wider community, has assessed or reassessed what it has to offer to that community and has in some cases reached a renewed understanding of its dependence upon, and its solidarity with, that community. Each, in its unique context, has set out to identify some of the things that local people need and some of the social and political issues affecting them. Each has attempted to maximise the potential for cooperation in and through meeting that need and addressing those issues. In each the resulting commitment to the well being of the community is changing the organisation.

ACTIVITIES BY BROAD AREA

The activities engaging the energies of around 2,000 volunteers from the twelve organisations examined include all age groups and range across the following broad areas:

- community support programmes;
- health programmes;
- social programmes;
- educational programmes;
- training programmes.

Community support programmes

Projects offer help in the sphere of community development, tackling crime, environmental issues, traffic calming, home safety and energy. They include community cafés and shops, playgroups and after school care, family support and meals on wheels. There are opportunities for art, drama and sport for all ages and abilities.

Health programmes

Projects range from services for people with mental illness to physically disabled people. They cover divorce, bereavement, respite for carers, women's issues, support for single parents and for senior citizens. Advice and counselling are available to people with problems relating to alcohol or other substance abuse.

Social programmes

Youth projects facilitate personal and social development for young people. Drop-in centres disseminate and exchange information and advice on welfare, housing and other problems. Accommodation is provided in hostels for homeless people or in newly built housing units. Emergency shelter and assistance with immediate needs are made available. Credit unions are in operation.

Educational programmes

Lifelong learning opportunities are provided and promoted. People with learning difficulties are encouraged and supported. There are parenting courses and homework clubs. Study groups address community reconciliation and social justice issues. Experiential learning opportunities are offered to volunteers.

Training programmes

IT training into jobs is provided, often for people on the margins of society, as part of what is in some cases an integrated strategy of economic regeneration.

ACTIVITIES BY SOCIAL CAPITAL DOMAIN

The report provides a discussion below of these examples of church-related voluntary action in terms of their contribution to the building of social cohesion through social capital formation. The significance of these activities comes sharply into relief when they are summarised and categorised under the eight domains of social capital drawn from the work of Forrest and Kearns (2001).

Empowerment

Amongst the twelve organisations studied are those:

- enlarging the range of channels for the empowerment of citizens, encouraging them to be more community oriented, cooperative and participative in ways that range from carrying out a community audit to involvement in management of church owned resources;

- providing access to ICT in order to connect individuals and strengthen community knowledge and sharing;
- developing locally appropriate programmes in support of welfare to work transitions and career guidance;
- channelling potential for credentialled educational attainment and jobs by alternative routes through education, business or community links;
- providing training and experience for parents in support of families, making parenting a more collective activity and enabling them to expand their social networks, often across the community divide;
- facilitating local business incubation and retail outlets.

Participation

Amongst the twelve organisations studied are those:

- strengthening actual and potential young offenders' positive social capital and raising their ambition through employment or volunteer placement;
- releasing and fostering artistic and creative gifts and providing a platform for their expression and celebration in the public space.

Associational activity and common purpose

Amongst the twelve organisations studied are those:

- facilitating lifelong learning, adult study groups, forums and circles, which include the work of peacebuilding and reconciliation across the community divide;
- ensuring the availability of primary health care and associated services.

Supporting networks and reciprocity

Amongst the twelve organisations studied are those:

- contributing to partnerships with other agencies working for community revitalisation and bringing national and international resources to bear on local issues;
- widening opportunities for young people to work alongside people from different social and ethnic backgrounds away from the home situation;
- setting up networks of street representatives.

Section 6 Findings

Collective norms and values

Amongst the twelve organisations studied are those:
- building local pride and rootedness and a sense of responsibility for, and ownership of, the quality of community life;
- promoting norms and values that discourage criminal behaviour in at risk young people.

Trust

Amongst the twelve organisations studied are those:
- extending potential for the loving relationships that stimulate children's physical, intellectual and emotional growth and positively influence their capacity to build trusting social relationships in later life;
- offering personal relationships that enhance the self-worth of young people through relationally based youth work and mentoring;
- reducing social distance and fostering inter personal trust.

Safety

Amongst the twelve organisations studied are those:

- making housing available;
- giving information and advice, food, financial assistance, temporary and long-term shelter, clothing, refuge from domestic violence;
- supporting those who are bereaved and those who have been traumatised;
- encouraging home safety and energy conservation schemes.

Belonging

Amongst the twelve organisations studied are those:

- breaking down a sense of isolation amongst older people and actively addressing threats to mental health;
- creating opportunities for young people in service learning and community volunteering;
- bringing the tangible assistance and care that begin to recreate a sense of well being and belonging to those who are socially excluded - disabled people, long-term unemployed people, those with criminal convictions, those suffering drug or alcohol abuse, those who are temporarily homeless;
- engaging in environmental improvement projects.

This is a picture of a large amount and variety of positive activity. The contribution of faith-based organisations to individuals, to the community and to society is a more complex story than can be told by listing what is measurable using quantitative data. This study demonstrates decisively that further and fuller investigation into the impact of such organisations is called for. Yet even a comprehensive and systematic quantitative mapping study of faith-related voluntary action throughout Northern Ireland would reveal only part of what there is to be told. Before this is illustrated from the interview findings some of the available statistics appearing in the profiles and cases above are brought together to give an estimation of the impact of these organisations.

WHO BENEFITS AND HOW

Flax Trust, largest of the FBOs examined, reported that 5,000 people had been through its training programme in the 25 years of its existence. There were 33 homeless families in its emergency housing units, more of which were planned. The drop-in centre provides places to 60 adolescents and young adults perceived as outside the main line in youth provision elsewhere. About 300 people in the neighbourhood receive meals each week and 3,000 are registered at the local health centre conceived and built through the trust's effort.

Oasis has trained 175 people through the government New Deal programme, 76 people in computer skills at various accredited levels and 48 women towards Open College Network certificates in a range of topics.

From its inception **Mornington** provided placements for 147 local people on government employment programmes. Some 196 employment trainees have passed through in the same period and, of these, 77 gained employment and 71 moved on to further education or training.

Barnabas saw its provision of work and training opportunities for 88 long-term unemployed people collapse with the demise of the ACE scheme. As it looked for ways to fill the gap, the trust continued preparing its 125 meals weekly and running the playgroup for the dozen or so special needs children.

The Shankill Parish Caring Association (**SPCA**) programme for seniors engaged 400 older people each week and 350 young people used the services of the youth team. A weeks-long project gathered 200 parents and children together in daily educational and recreational activities.

Section 6 Findings

YMCA statistics showed that the organisation involved more than 38,300 people over the whole island of Ireland. Some 8,500 young people aged between 7 and 25 years are enrolled in the 13 local associations across Northern Ireland and, if the report of the general inspection is to be believed, participate 'fully and with a real sense of enjoyment' (Education and Training Inspectorate, 2002, 3.4).
These figures, coming from organisations accountable to outside funding agencies, are on record. Coming through in the interviews are facts of another kind however, equally real but not recorded in numerical form. They also tell of the impact of the work of the FBOs in the study. Often they come from church congregations. Frequently they are indicative of benefits flowing beyond the membership into the surrounding community.

A respondent from **Ballysillan** observed that over the years a high proportion of Boys' Brigade members had obtained Duke of Edinburgh awards and other awards relating to civic responsibility and entered careers in public service. Another aspect of this church, 'just something that is encouraged' is the reported regular involvement of youth club members in activities to raise money for what are considered to be worthy causes in the local community.

At **Holy Family**, the leadership team set aside the usual assumption that every Catholic within the parish boundary was a member. They carried out an audit of the population that included an invitation to return a form indicating a desire to be on a list of active members. The fact that almost eight thousand people did so may be interpreted in several ways. One of them must be that, for some people at least, there were benefits from doing so. Among them might be a pioneering programme devised by staff in one of the parish schools. Sixty children who had failed the 11+ examination were enrolled for GNVQs thanks to a course that had attracted widespread interest from educationalists.

Members of **Knocknagoney** congregation found that 700 households in their local area had little access to social, educational or leisure facilities. They shared their buildings through a management committee consisting of members from both the congregation and the local community council. The committee then programmed activities for the benefit of the whole community.

Shared premises were also a feature of **Shankill** parish in Lurgan. Use of one of its buildings was recorded as 96 percent community and 4 percent parish activity.

Methodist City Mission in Derry incorporated its dedicated space for worship within a building designed for mixed use by groups, including local businesses and statutory bodies, and managed by a committee comprising representatives of the congregation and other user groups. The reported daily weekday number of people passing through the building (259 - 403) reflects a high level of local ownership. This is perhaps due in part to the already established tradition of social outreach and community involvement of the organisation in the area through its hostel for homeless men. It may also reflect the wide consultation process in connection with the new building designed to be open and available to all for practical assistance in the form of benefit advice along with food and clothing, facilities and recreation, social solidarity and companionship. The new building has itself been welcomed as a hopeful sign in its neighbourhood. It is recognised as a visible focus for continuing cross-community, peace and reconciliation efforts and a place where no one is stigmatised by entering.

The community worker at **Benmoe** spoke about the stirring of a revived community spirit evidenced by the general street clean up on a housing estate.

There was benefit also to the organisations themselves, to their members, to the staff employed and to those who volunteered their time and energy.

Staff in **Holy Family** and in **Shankill** spoke of the personal growth experienced by those members who 'took responsibility' and 'exercised a ministry' in their churches. The bundle of energy, expertise and experience they represented was 'exciting to work with'.

A volunteer at **Barnabas** in Enniskillen spoke about the training that she had undergone, and about the resulting sense of achievement and the continuing satisfaction both from her work and from being one of a team of people for whom she had a high regard. This was echoed at **Oasis** in Belfast, where the leader singled out the quality and commitment of the staff as a particular strength of his organisation.

A similar regard for one another was very obvious in the greetings, the body language and the formal speeches when the trustees, staff, volunteers and members of the **Omagh** Boys and Girls Club met for the ceremony to mark the opening of a new base for their activities.

A member at **Knocknagoney** referred to her pride at being associated with what was happening at the church and at the way in which the community's perception of the congregation had been changed since the management and use of the church facilities had been shared.

A similar sense of movement was experienced at **Benmoe**, where the action taken by this congregation encouraged a degree of risk taking by others and proved to be a catalyst for changing the community's regard for all of the churches in the local area.

Clearly then there are benefits flowing from the activities outlined above. They flow to the members. They flow beyond the membership into the surrounding community and this is important. But in Northern Ireland the surrounding community can still be 'our' community as opposed to 'their' community, with the benefits simply reinforcing the sense of difference. It is when benefits are seen to cross this division that the important becomes more significant.

CROSS-COMMUNITY BENEFIT

The study found that churches were being perceived in a new light by people in their localities. In each congregation, the church's self-perception was also in the process of change. One minister spoke of 'the struggle to find a new way of being church'. Without exception each leader reported how, directly or obliquely, they had addressed the question of what they were 'actually for'. The process had brought with it a recognition of the church as embedded in the community, an acknowledgment of the place of others in the community and an opening up to new connections and collaborations. This in turn demanded that, where this was not already in place, the church members explore possibilities for developing a cross-community dimension as part of their work. In some areas this carried the danger of alienating a proportion of the existing membership or bringing unwelcome attention from local paramilitaries. A minister admitted that 'for the present, the congregation could not be said to be actively challenging the lines of difference and division'. Where there was evidence that the challenge had been set out, respondents were cautious about any exposure of the details of their activities in this area.

For one minister cross-community work was something focused in 'activities below the line of sight'. Another quoted from a church document, saying that, while there was no specific or self-conscious cross-community programme in his congregation, 'in many instances meeting over a bowl of soup at a community luncheon club will be much less threatening than coming together for a planned discussion on cross-community co-operation, and in the long run it may be more effective'.

The churches were alive to the issue and none restricted its voluntary welfare activities to its own side of the religious divide, though the groups engaging in boundary crossing activities were often self-selecting. Every minister encouraged members of the congregation to build good personal links across the community divide even if this was not a formal objective of the organisation. One spoke of politically sensitive ongoing contacts. Another, perhaps because of the success of its projects, the sheer numbers involved and the fact that his church had openly faced down internal criticism, was unapologetic about its programmes being open to all comers. In fact it had formed a charitable trust in order to further precisely this kind of work. This points up the key fact that what was difficult for churches was often less so for the para-churches with their greater independence and more focused purposes.

SPCA, Shankill Parish Caring Association in Lurgan, had developed innovative ideas in youth and children's work, bringing in people from all backgrounds. The PAKT concept (Parents And Kids Together) that originated there, concentrating on relationships between children and parents within the family, was specifically designed to cross both the generation gap and community divisions. The Jethro Project was similarly intended to cross the gap between communities in Lurgan.

The founders of **Flax** in Belfast intended that it should engage directly with the social and economic causes of intercommunity hatred and violence. Out of a largely Catholic community that had been politicised and unified by the experiences of the late 1960s and early 1970s came an organisation whose explicit aim was to contribute to social justice and reconciliation. That intention was expressed in a way that attracted funding from 63 agencies and attracted a range of commercial partners. From the beginning the board was made up of a religiously mixed body of people. The business incubation enterprise drew 60 percent of its clients from the Protestant community. The training programmes that had placed 5,000 people in employment were equally to the benefit of each community. Their partnership across the religious divide with the Salvation Army made newly built supported housing units available for elderly people. It also offered emergency and short-term accommodation for homeless families and single women who could then be resettled through the Army's rehabilitation and training programme. On the cultural community side of things at Flax, the arts centre, with its theatre, dance studio and gallery, was used as a vehicle for inter-

Section 6 Findings

community reconciliation. The community association had a cross-community group overseeing services to disabled people, single parents and senior citizens, including preparation and delivery of meals on wheels to any in the neighbourhood who needed them. There were cross border contacts in place and a women's forum had produced a publication written from both Catholic and Protestant viewpoints.

At the **Omagh** club, the board was made up of 5 Catholic and 4 Protestant people. The leader indicated that their policy required all activities and programmes to demonstrate a cross-community dimension. These activities were not all as intentional as the twelve week module that drew religiously mixed groups together in an exploration of identity. Some had developed naturally over time through the strong links existing with schools, with Protestant youth clubs and with mixed sporting networks. This FBO had begun originally as a club mainly for the young people of a Catholic parish in the town but was open to others. More recently, and especially since the indiscriminate bombing of the town centre in 1998, there was a new determination to cross the line of division and to be of benefit to the whole community. Clear signs of such a sense of determination and obligation were in evidence at the opening ceremony for the club's new building in 2001. Choirs from the Catholic primary and the county primary entertained a large gathering of members, friends, dignitaries and supporters from near and far. The Catholic priest and the local Methodist minister offered prayers. A young woman, just through her first year at university, spoke of what the club had meant to her in her formative years. A speech reflected on the club's new home, the Station Centre, and the significance of its siting on an old railway yard from which some of the stones for its building had come. The old town station was described, perhaps a little lyrically, as

> *a place where all the people of Omagh met to travel to explore new horizons and to seek adventure. It was a place where they returned home in happy times, sometimes in sadness. I see each of those stones belonging to every street, avenue, park in the Omagh area. They are cemented together to keep the structure strong, durable, unbreakable. My hope is that the work in the Station Centre will provide the cement to bring our community together, particularly our young people. The Station Centre belongs to all of the citizens of Omagh and district. If we are truly interested in that vibrant healthy democracy, then we must strive to make the Station Centre totally inclusive, a focal point for the whole community* (McMahon, 2001).

The work of **Barnabas** was also galvanised by tragedy. The leader explained how a bomb detonated at a Remembrance Day ceremony in Enniskillen in 1987 that killed 11 people had energised the team that encouraged the rebuilding of trust and drove a determination to provide opportunities for people to come together across the divide. Subsequent funding vicissitudes meant that they were rethinking their operation at the time of the study, but the facility they ran for young people proved to be a base for socialising that was acceptable to unattached youth of different backgrounds. And the leadership's awareness of a high proportion of elderly isolated people in the population, gained through the network of Methodist churches in the surrounding countryside, led to a programme of regular supportive contact from a team of volunteers at the trust.

YMCA actively promotes cross-community participation and encounter at all levels in all activities. The National Council set community relations as a major focus of its work for over a decade and the organisation has transformed itself from what was perceived as a mainly Protestant and male body into a more inclusive one with a high profile for promoting anti-sectarian values. Innovative programmes have drawn participants from differing religious backgrounds in Northern Ireland. National and international programmes have brought many young people together to examine issues around diversity and mutual understanding. National Council staff train local association staff in the development of strategies for embedding the concepts of equity, diversity and interdependence into their programme and, in this way, to increase the involvement of young people in community relations work. For a local association to be set up there must be a request from church people in the area with a concern for the welfare of young people and a manifest willingness to come together with others to discuss these issues from a faith base. YMCA (Central) helps to identify needs and possible responses, then decides whether to place a development officer in the location to build the constituency. A management group, which must be cross-community in composition, is set up and people are required to commit themselves to working for the success of the enterprise.

Oasis emerged from a congregation of people unwilling to be identified with Catholic or Protestant church stereotypes. The parent Christian Fellowship Church congregation provides core staff, volunteers and ongoing strong moral support for this organisation's work to bring together people from different backgrounds, life experiences and viewpoints. Based within a largely Protestant area of the city, Oasis has good contacts with community workers and associations in Catholic areas, both nearby and across Belfast. Such contact facilitates cross-community work with groups of women and of young people. It also enables cooperative training links. There is also a pilot befriending scheme, integrated with and aiming to complement the work of general practitioners and community practice nurses in the area. In the context of continuing troubles-related tension this scheme, designed to give more time to people's anxieties than the health professionals could offer, represents an important contribution to the social fabric.

Mornington is rooted in a neighbourhood of Belfast from which a group of people initiated action on behalf of their own unemployed young people. The first director to be appointed, who is still in post, built on this when he committed himself to living within the immediate area, bringing his family with him. Over time people from a range of religious backgrounds gravitated towards the work, some of them relinquishing their existing church membership and identifying with the resulting community of interest. The deep engagement of such people, often from a Protestant background, was accepted in this now predominantly Catholic area. Firmly committed to a community development approach, Mornington has raised the profile of faith throughout the range of its activities at the request of local people. In so doing it creates new opportunities for people of differing religions to come together in a safe place in order to get to know something about their range of viewpoints. This FBO devised a model of practice, making its experience in cross-community approaches available to other interested organisations, particularly churches both across Belfast and in several nearby towns.

COMMUNITY COHESION AND SOCIAL CAPITAL FORMATION

Social cohesion has long been an issue of concern in social policy thinking. As 'community cohesion' it came under recent examination through the Home Office enquiry into factors that lay behind serious disturbances in towns and cities in England in the late spring of 2001. The report of the resulting Independent Review Team (Home Office, 2001), acknowledged some difficulty with definition. Its analysis of the concept borrowed Canadian Government usage of the term:

> *The ongoing process of developing a community of shared values, shared challenges and equal opportunity within Canada, based on a sense of trust, hope and reciprocity among all Canadians* (Social Cohesion Network, 1997).

It barely takes the substitution of Northern Ireland for Canada for it to be very clear indeed that questions raised of social capital apply with equal force to the concept of community cohesion. In a society that is fundamentally split, cohesion may be an admirable aspiration, but it may not always be a positive attribute. For beyond the central split, in a patchwork of communities that operate on a sense of fear and distrust of the other, individual people may well be integrated into local ethnic or religion-based communities that are in turn divided from other communities. So the cohesion that is desirable is one that requires participation across the confines of local communities, knitting them together into a wider whole. Building local community cohesion may in fact be at the cost of a sense of trust and common purpose throughout wider society.

In their exploration of the relationship between wider societal cohesion and the strength of locally based communities, Ray Forrest and Ade Kearns examine the interaction between social cohesion and social capital (Forrest & Kearns, 2001). Their intention is to break down these two closely linked concepts for policy action. They identify five domains of social cohesion. These are

- common values and a civic culture;
- social order and social control;
- social solidarity and reductions in wealth disparities;
- social networks and social capital;
- place attachment and identity.

Thus they see the idea of social capital located within the broader notion of social cohesion. Their approach is followed here insofar as the faith-related voluntary action discovered by this project is examined for both social capital forming and social cohesion building dimensions. The social capital forming dimension here means activity that fits within the description of the eight domains of social capital identified in the work of Forrest and Kearns as they appear in the table below.

Section 6 Findings

Table 6. The domains of social capital (Forrest and Kearns, 2001)

Domain	Description
Empowerment	That people feel they have a voice which is listened to; are involved in processes that affect them; can themselves take action to initiate changes
Participation	That people take part in social and community activities; local events occur and are well attended
Associational activity and common purpose	That people co-operate with one another through the formation of formal and informal groups to further their interests
Supporting networks and reciprocity	That individuals and organisations co-operate to support one another for either mutual or one-sided gain; an expectation that help would be given to or received from others when needed
Collective norms and values	That people share common values and norms of behaviour
Trust	That people feel they can trust their co-residents and local organisations responsible for governing or serving their area
Safety	That people feel safe in their neighbourhood and are not restricted in their use of public space by fear
Belonging	That people feel connected to their co-residents, their home area, have a sense of belonging to the place and its people

Benmoe: social cohesion is under threat in the part of town where Benmoe is located. Problems associated with anti social behaviour, drug trafficking and intimidation have contributed to the weakening of community spirit. Sectarianism adds to an atmosphere in which one housing estate has become a place where few people want to live. Local groups seemed to be individually too weak to respond constructively. The Housing Executive is demolishing dwellings instead of building them. Statutory services are perceived as having 'given up'. Members of this congregation, seeking ways in which to engage with this situation, looked around for allies amongst other local churches and opened themselves up to wider potential linkages. One result is a long-term commitment to work towards a shared project of community building. What is envisaged, a number of houses for owner occupation built through Habitat for Humanity, means that people will have to be convinced that the neighbourhood is a good one in which to live. This in turn implies a serious attempt by this FBO and its allies to turn back the tide of social decline.

The people of this congregation, through their bonding social capital, have come together with a strong sense of identity and purpose. Bridging social capital is also important in their case, enabling them to begin to collaborate with churches and other organisations in the local partnership. They found support and they negotiated shared understanding through horizontal linkages that have become as real to them, practically speaking, as the vertical structures of their own denomination. This discovery triggered a balance of bonding and bridging social capital that fostered respect between those within, and those outside, the church family. As reported by the community worker, members of this congregation showed a willingness to be exploratory, honest about failure and ready to improvise. In the relationships and patterns of trust that developed through Benmoe's 'Shebeg' pastoral centre, social capital provided for residents of the neighbourhood a way in to cultural, human and economic capital (Schneider, 2001).

Shankill Parish Caring Association, Lurgan: during the 1990s SPCA had implemented some innovative ideas in areas of youth and children's work, the impact of which were felt throughout the town and beyond. For example, early working parents with no family in the town could leave children for breakfast and have them looked after at their own club when school ended. The pioneering cross-community PAKT concept, concentrating on relationships between children and parents within the family unit, was demonstrably important both for the families and for social cohesion. Large numbers are involved. The activities for all ages and the facilities made available for everyone's use on church premises touch many people in every quarter of the town. Much of the work of this FBO attracts people from both Protestant and Catholic backgrounds and here, as in several of the organisations, social capital is linked in an enabling way to human capital creation. Learning is promoted as an acceptable and enjoyable activity. There are opportunities for informal modes of learning and for developing the skills acquired through learning by doing. From children's work to the seniors' groups people deploy their skills and talents. The organisations provide access to important information and ideas, many of them with high levels of cross-cutting ties.

Oasis, Belfast: this is true also for Oasis. In addition linking social capital plays a part in enabling a process of learning from the practice of more experienced faith-based community development groups elsewhere in the UK. It has also brought into play significant funding that has in turn enabled new forms of social association and learning through the use of information technology. Through this, and through fostering innovative recruitment practices on the part of some major employers with whom it has developed partnerships, Oasis has used linking social capital to create bridging social capital between those who were excluded from and those who were rich in work and resources.

Flax, Belfast, pushes even further with linking social capital enabling extensive commercial interests, business incubation, work preparation schemes and training and support packages aimed at those most in need. Its move into the provision of housing along with the Salvation Army has made it a significant player in the field. Its creation of a shopping complex, with the added attraction of a health centre, in an area hitherto badly served provides a focal point of increased opportunity for local entrepreneurs. The trust has arguably done something to mitigate a sense of injustice amongst a population that perceived itself as marginalised. A determination to see justice and to combat alienation and despair underlay the beginnings of this FBO (Turley & Kavanagh, 1990). Bonding social capital continues to help them tackle their sense of exclusion and oppression through preserving culture and providing informal support mechanisms. It has generated strong local institutions that enhance the people's self esteem and encourage civic participation and vigorous representation at City Hall level. As to bridging social capital, on both local community issues and on the wider business front the organisation has made its cross-cutting links more than just paper connections. Its beginnings included a street collection that became known as the 'Mars Bar Fund', so called because it asked of each household the price of a bar of chocolate each week. This mobilised enough volunteers to cover the parish, door-to-door, every week. It engaged the interest and the contribution of a huge proportion of the local population and through it they generated financial leverage in pursuit of their vision. Flax has grown to the point where it is collaborating with other interests across Northern Ireland in the creation of a community bank.

At **Omagh Boys and Girls Club** the management had proved themselves by building up capacity and establishing the credentials of the club over time. Those guiding the organisation forward were in the main people who had grown up in the town and who had themselves been members in younger days. They were known to be serious in their intent to cross the community divide. This had been recognised both by the agencies that backed the enterprise financially and by the people from the Protestant community who had joined the trustees. Respondents spoke of considerable trust amongst the core group and, particularly since the Omagh atrocity in 1998, a sense of obligation towards the whole town to make a success of the organisation as a bridge and the centre as a meeting place for all people and traditions. They showed a determination to extend a sense of ownership beyond the immediate locality. And while one board member, a local clergyman, conceded that not every Protestant might yet be likely to feel totally comfortable in the club, he was confident about the direction that the club was taking as this new chapter in its history opened up. The board were working hard to find ways of ensuring that the ethos within the new building was one in which people of any background could feel welcome and at home.

YMCA (National) works hard to reach the most alienated and vulnerable young people, to improve their self-confidence, introduce them to others from a wide variety of social, cultural and geographical backgrounds and present them with opportunities to gain knowledge, skills and expertise. With a high level of professional youth work skills, the team is known for its ability to establish and sustain positive relationships with young people. The members use a community development approach, working in partnership with local associations to enable them to develop their own action plans and objectives and draw on the extensive YMCA network for support. The YMCA approach to family youth work that is used by local associations throughout Ireland is based upon the PAKT model, originally developed in Shankill parish with telling impact on social cohesion in Lurgan.

LEADERSHIP, FUNDING AND FRAGILITY

> *Social capital is not something which can be instantly created, or very rapidly created. Its accumulation, and its erosion, is a process which almost always requires several years at least. It therefore acts as an important counterweight to the tendency to look for quick fix solutions* (Schuller, 2000, p. 6).

Section 6 Findings

A long-term perspective is a distinctive mark of the people in leadership of the twelve FBOs in this study. They are aware that change comes slowly. In para-church organisations the question of the appropriate pace of change can lead to problems with funders who may want to see short-term results. In parishes and congregations change at any pace is not always welcome. Rarely does the sustainability of the operation depend on funding per se. The quality of leadership and the interaction between leaders and led plays a large, if not a crucial part. Leadership and funding together tell a story of sustainability or of fragility.

In the case of **YMCA (National)** organisational authority and control are limited. National Council equates to the headquarters of what is a federated movement, that is one in which there is a bottom-up relationship between local and central units (Young, 1989). The structure is one in which the central body is controlled to some extent by the units which enter voluntarily into the larger association. Progress is made through subtle persuasion and a leadership style that encourages consultation and progress towards consensus. While a para-church might be considered to hold a common belief system, set of values and goals, YMCA (National Council) relates to a range of diverse local groups operating within the two different socio-cultural and religio-political contexts of Ireland, north and south. Cast in the role of defining and symbolising what the movement is about and of undertaking activity that can provide a sense of purpose, it is not easy for it in these circumstances to forge a sense of unity and direction for the future. Much depends on leadership helping associations to develop their own initiative and strengthening them in the use of their own judgement in a way that leaves them with actual ownership and control of the process of risk and change.

Leadership gifts noted in the interviews included that of imaginative vision and the ability to inspire people to use their own gifts to the full, giving them the freedom they needed to do things their way and persuading those with power of their common interest in the success of the enterprise. The vision grows out of local experience in each case. It is not decided and asserted or imposed from elsewhere. It is discovered and accepted within each context. One respondent spoke of his organisation's leader as 'inspirational' and the 'vision keeper'. Such qualities found public expression in words spoken, and greeted with approbation, at ceremonies in Omagh, Belfast and Derry to open new buildings attended by the researcher. At **Knocknagoney** and at **City Mission** there were references to the capacity of leadership to 'keep the vision alive', to promote the project across professional networks, to drive it through to completion as a visible focus for the whole community.

There is an enabling and collaborative dimension to leadership, one that speaks of everyone learning to exercise his or her gifts and seeks their active input. The way in which **Shankill** departments of ministry were established and the incorporation of a pastoral council into the team at **Holy Family** were just two examples. The Shankill leadership introduced a structured course called Network that guided over a hundred people through a process of discovering their own gifts and deciding what they could contribute to the purposes of the organisation. Members of Holy Family were encouraged to be involved in taking responsibility for the praying, caring and community-building mission of the organisation and were reported as 'more than ever' doing so.

The capacity to see difficulties as new possibilities, to turn crises into opportunities and to encourage new thinking is also in evidence. The parish administrator at **Holy Family**, referring to the diminishing number of vocations to the priesthood, saw this shortage as driving a process of change. 'There'll be fewer priests. But God's grace is working to make people take responsibility and exercise their ministry as the baptised', he said. Demographic change in Lurgan resulted in the **Shankill** congregation meeting for worship in a building that was perceived to be in what had become 'Catholic territory'. This reality, which was thrown into relief by local civil unrest, sharpened the question of what the congregation's role was to be in the town. This enabled the leadership to stimulate new thinking about responsibilities for serious engagement with the community at large. The formation of **SPCA** as a company limited by guarantee allowed it to access funding for initiatives in social action, community development and cross-community work like the Community Bridges project and the Jethro Centre. The **Knocknagoney** experience could be read as one of leadership turning weakness into strength through encouraging dialogue between members of the congregation and people in the local community. Through a process of meeting to share concerns about the neighbourhood the congregation began to see itself in a new light, to understand its place in, and its value to, the community in a new way. It made a conscious decision to look for ways of cooperating with the local community and it successfully argued its case with denominational authorities that owned the church premises.

Benmoe took a different path, but was stimulated by a similar sense of weakness as people moved out of what they saw as a declining area. The situation had allowed the leadership to ask fundamental questions about the purpose of the organisation and how it related to the community of which they were part. The result was a decision to adopt what has been called the 'project model' of mission,

Section 6 Findings 141

delegating key priorities to a semi-independent organisation (Wells, 2001b). There were tensions of course and not everyone in the congregation expressed the same commitment to the project. Indeed there was a flourishing traditional dimension to congregational life, with organisations holding appeal for insiders rather than outsiders. Some older members thought of the centre as a matter of mission in the sense of evangelism and numbers converted or souls saved. Others expressed great interest in how work was actually going and how the community worker managed in the face of the pressures. Part of the leadership task was to hold these differing understandings together and to encourage the widest possible ownership of the work.

Similar leadership qualities and similar tensions were in evidence at **Ballysillan**, where the minister spoke of one of the strengths of local churches, namely a commitment to remaining in the area through thick and thin. He saw such commitment as something that allowed a strategic approach to deepening the engagement of the congregation with the local community. The current approach was through relational youth work from a dedicated base on the congregation's premises. This was understood and supported by some members. Others saw any attempt at building bridges with community as inappropriate. Holding the two groups together, encouraging acceptance of other viewpoints while remaining clear-sighted about priorities, was a challenge to leadership.

There was another kind of challenge facing the leadership of **Barnabas**. Here the facilities at the purpose-built premises were both an asset and a liability. The leader reported a 'lack of adequate funds' for upkeep of the building and for running services at previous levels possible through the ACE scheme. The transition to New Deal arrangements, reducing the scope of the organisation's activities, coincided with a change in other circumstances that had made possible the genesis of Barnabas from within the Methodist congregation. A group of people with the expertise, skills and contacts to turn the church's hopes of social action into reality had reached a critical stage in their planning when the terrorist atrocity at the cenotaph on Remembrance Day 1987 left Enniskillen reeling. The resulting groundswell of feeling, allied perhaps to international media attention, brought people closer together and engendered a sense that something should be done as 'a living memorial' to those who had been killed and injured. Barnabas Trust was born. With the eventual dissipation of that early energy and goodwill, with the changed government funding package insufficient to cover costs, with the departure of some of the original planning team and the impact on the morale of the staff and volunteers, the leadership of this FBO was reassessing the operation in order to find a way to strengthen links with the parent congregation and move forward.

Despite the tensions noted above, the link between congregation and project is strong at **Benmoe**, where an appropriate distance is maintained operationally, yet where the congregation has taken complete responsibility for funding the work and is unwilling to surrender the direction of its policy to the demands of any outside funding agency. **Oasis**, after a decade in existence, with its own legal standing and its work firmly established, has attracted major funding. The leadership team was perceived by one respondent as friendly and welcoming, enthusiastic and open, appreciative of the individuality of all those with whom they dealt. Backed by the active concern of a support team in the congregation out of which Oasis originally grew, they reported a lack of staff to meet the extra demands of new projects. In addition they felt themselves to be poor at marketing the project and uncomfortable with public relations. Their ongoing problem is that of finding the time and energy for seeking funding sources. Funders are seen as looking for novel short-term projects. The policy of Oasis is to embark on deliberate action in response to clear local need. It therefore looks for longer-term underpinning.

Problems arising from a short-term funding regime were identified in the report of the Education and Training Inspectorate on **YMCA**. It is a challenge also for **Mornington**. Further, one of the very features contributing to Mornington's local credibility, namely a 'non glossy image', possibly weakened its competitiveness in attracting funding in the changed climate. As with Barnabas, changes in government funding policy and the demise of the ACE scheme make it difficult to sustain work training programmes and community services. With no parent congregation from which to seek support, Mornington turned to its roots in the neighbourhood. At another level, **Flax** was at a point where it had developed a critical mass and momentum all of its own. A flair for strategic planning and social entrepreneurship characterised the leadership. Its community activities remained anchored in the local, but its business interests had developed an international profile.

The research did not enquire directly into how the leaders of these organisations consider the community engagement aspect of their work could be made more effective, inclusive and sustainable. The difficulty of access to funding, already a critical matter in the experience of some grassroots FBOs in the London boroughs (Peake, 2001), did however emerge as an issue. Not all of the twelve organisations expressed interest in government funding. Fears of goal displacement and loss of ownership and independence were expressed by the ministers of some congregations. Others considered that it would stabilise, enhance and enable their work. To give FBOs that want it greater access to government funding could, of course, risk overestimating what they are capable of sustaining. It could also support social capital formation of a bonding and exclusive kind resulting in strengthened local cohesion at the expense of wider allegiance. Arguably any support from public funds offered to faith-based organisations should be conditional upon demonstrable public benefit. In the context of Northern Ireland where, rightly or wrongly, the churches are generally perceived to look after their own, the focus would be directed towards the rights and responsibilities that all citizens have in common and away from sectional interest. Any application for funding would include an explicit intention to build a sense of trust and common purpose across the religious divide.

Whether self supporting or funded from outside, the twelve organisations examined here depend greatly upon their leadership to be carriers of a compelling vision that attracts others, motivates them and captures their trust. Through their own commitment the leaders exemplify what the organisation stands for as well as what it does. No matter whether the organisation is church or para-church, hierarchical or more democratic, leadership seems to be most successful when it:

- takes the long perspective on change;
- combines a flair for strategic planning with a willingness to take risks;
- stimulates new thinking and opens up to new collaboration;
- trusts other players, inspiring and enabling their contribution;
- holds the ground through tensions and crises.

The spectrum of voluntary activity in which these churches and faith-based organisations are engaged goes beyond traditional services for church members to include building local rootedness and pride in community life, enlarging channels for the empowerment of all citizens and contributing to partnerships with other agencies working for community revitalisation. This makes them more than self or mutual benefit organisations. They are moving beyond the churches' position as representatives of ethnic loyalty and markers of separatist communities in Northern Ireland. They are taking risks to do so against an apparent background of little official interest by denominations in experimentation or in specialist ministries of the kind more taken for granted elsewhere in the United Kingdom. With the traditional models of ministry no longer working as they once did and the churches' central bodies showing little sign of equipping themselves to offer incisive support, these organisations show the marks of a serious attempt to meet the demands of a world conditioned by today's realities. In most cases they are giving expression to their values in a way that makes an impact upon the specifics of local issues and cleavages, local lives and needs. Their story is one of commitment, risk and trust. The social capital that they generate in the course of their spiritual and practical activities is embedded in networks that have a presence in every community on the island of Ireland with well developed cross border national structures as well as extensive international links. They have leaders who live in the community they serve; they have a range of specialists upon whom they may call and they have their own financial resources. With their values driving a concern for issues that government has a duty to address, they comprise significant networks and key sources of social capital that is available for wider use. One hopes that the policy significance of this will not be lost on those who are charged with a responsibility to facilitate neighbourhood regeneration in Northern Ireland.

SECTION 7   DISCUSSION AND CONCLUSIONS

The section acknowledges the limited capacity of churches and other faith-based organisations to influence the huge forces at work in society in Northern Ireland. It points nevertheless to evidence of their tenacity and a commitment that

- stems from and builds upon religious values;
- is willing to take risks;
- fosters a positive and people centred approach to regeneration;
- drives a dynamic that encourages social capital formation.

The research project has found that church-related voluntary action is of benefit not just to church members, but to the well being of society at large. However a job remains to be done on changing misperceptions of the work of such bodies in Northern Ireland. Further research is imperative.

The section sets out key findings under each of the twelve profile headings and then proceeds to trace some of the ways in which the organisations in the study demonstrate resilience and persistence in the face of difficulty. It locates these qualities in the faith base of the organisations and briefly notes the resonances between religious values and the elements of social capital. The discussion returns to policy issues, contrasting developments in Britain with the absence of movement in Northern Ireland. The section ends with some recommendations for moving the dialogue forward.

KEY FINDINGS

Type of faith-based organisation

From small congregations to large para-churches, faith-based organisations (FBOs) are to be found in a striking range of forms and types in Northern Ireland. They are usually embedded in the community and not staffed and administered from outside as are statutory agencies.

Objectives

The objectives of churches and other FBOs are variously expressed but usually involve an intent to change human lives and conditions for the better. They exhibit value commitments that are of enormous social significance.

Activities

A huge diversity of activities, services and facilities is made available through churches and FBOs both for members and for people outside the membership circle. By such means these organisations form and sustain significant reserves of social capital that are available to the local community.

Buildings

The premises used by churches and FBOs are often important sites for civic engagement in local communities.

Participation

Programmes run by churches and FBOs are supported by large numbers of volunteers, of whom many see such voluntary activity as a practical expression of their faith. The spiritual dimension to their existence provides an underpinning to their practical work. The faith base adds urgency to social commitment and plays a part in motivating the 2000 volunteers at work in the 12 organisations investigated in this project.

Resourcing and use of research

The churches and FBOs examined here have considerable financial, human and physical resources. They need a greater appreciation of the value of research in enabling the most effective and efficient use of their resources.

Linkages

There is evidence that churches and FBOs may be opening up to a greater awareness of the value of working cooperatively and in partnership with other bodies. Some unexpected and positive collaborative relationships are in place through their bridging and linking social capital. Where shared concern leads to

Section 7 Discussion and Conclusions

united local effort by churches, denominational boundaries become less significant.

Cross-community dimension

There is universal recognition of the importance of this dimension in the context of Northern Ireland and some courageous steps have been taken by the churches and FBOs in the study. They serve to highlight the need for further imaginative action to contribute towards wider social cohesion. Three quarters of the survey respondents said that the churches should be doing much more to improve community relations.

Flexibility

These organisations demonstrate considerable flexibility and imagination in their responses to local conditions. However all responses seem to have begun from a deliberate attempt to look carefully at, and identify with, the local community, to listen to local expression of need and to decide how best to stimulate local action to address that need. In some cases this is by direct provision of services or facilities. In some it is by facilitating provision by other agencies.

Social inclusion and social cohesion

These organisations are making serious attempts to reach the most marginalised and vulnerable people in local communities. They are doing so in a way that both contributes to an improvement in people's material conditions and nurtures the heart of the community.

Dissolving stereotypes

The case studies present a picture of organisations that have moved beyond the received view of the churches as representatives of ethnic loyalty and markers of separatist communities. Complementing these findings are the responses from the survey which show members of the organisations as people who have a strong sense of belonging to their church and are often active in other local organisations. They are themselves more concerned to respond to people in need than to add to their church's membership. They want the church to be a compassionate community partner, to care for human wellbeing and to assist neighbourhood development.

Leadership

The quality of leadership in each church or faith-based organisation is crucial for shaping the direction and strength of its voluntary engagement.

CHURCHES AND COMMITMENT, RISK AND TRUST

In the area of North Belfast where **Flax Trust** enables so much that is positive and where, close by, the **Ballysillan** youth project goes about its cross-cutting work, Ardoyne has been the focal point for an outflowing of increasing bitterness and social disintegration that has not yet been staunched. Throughout the autumn of 2001 and 2002 news media carried the story of terrified children on their daily walk to school. Tensions remain. This single example of life at the interface serves to put the work of faith-based organisations in perspective. It is a sobering thought that the same point might be illustrated within or close by the location of virtually every FBO in the study. In the light of this, a degree of realism is appropriate when considering the capacity of such organisations, or indeed the utility of social capital (see Appendix I), to offer much leverage on the formidable forces at work in society in Northern Ireland.

> *It will take at least half a generation to repair something that has been destroyed in Northern Ireland. We just keep chipping away. That's how it is ...*
>
> *We think in terms of building community and not just chasing funds for community buildings. It's a long haul.*

These are the words of two of the ministers in the study. Other leaders made similar statements. They are realistic without being fatalistic. They also carry a hope that is more than a sunny optimism. It comes through in words from a grant application made by a Belfast FBO:

> *We have a commitment to maintaining and developing our explicit desire to stay in the city, and to do what we can to influence the present and future generations .... our thinking derives from a substantial theological base, and not from a transient whim or perceived opportunism.*

Section 7 Discussion and Conclusions

It is important to give that theological base its place. John Hickey, writing about the effect of religious belief on the conflict in Northern Ireland, makes the point that there is

> *a reluctance among social scientists to accept the concept of commitment, or the ensuing fact that people are capable of ordering their actions on the basis of commitment. It is strange that this should be so when there is so much evidence to support a counter position* (Hickey, 1984, p. 80).

One social scientist made much of just such a piece of evidence. For an ethnographic study of a 'small, essentially American, essentially Christian group engaged in community revitalization in a totally Malay, totally Muslim village in the late 1970s', he noted how much personal sacrifice some people will endure out of a commitment to others who are disadvantaged. He illustrated the depth of the commitment of the volunteers with the observation that they refrained from celebrating the faith that directed most of them there in the first place. Their aim was to get villagers to appreciate what they could do for themselves. In order to gain access to the village to pursue this aim, 'the would-be changers changed themselves instead in order to ensure that their target group remained unchanged'. This was what he described as 'the most incredible aspect' of their effort (Wolcott, 1994, p. 216).

Evidence from the churches and para-churches in Northern Ireland that were examined in this research project suggests that a similar quality is to be found in some of the people in the province's faith communities. For example, the pastoral centre at **Benmoe** is putting the resources of the congregation at the service of the local area in a way that respects local people. It is a process of trust building that requires restraint on the part of the worker, the volunteers and the congregation. There is a sense of Wolcott's observation of people changing themselves so as not to change others. **Oasis** is also building trust in a way that reflects a commitment to change its approach as it learns from local people and from its own mistakes. In a part of Belfast that is struggling to recover from the loss of shipbuilding and its associated trades, the way in which Oasis was seen to go about establishing a presence in the neighbourhood was appreciated. Their initial project came to nothing. The Oasis team thought again, and again they failed. But they were seen to learn from their failure and not to give up. Through the dialogue they developed with statutory bodies in the area, with local groups and individual people and with FBOs elsewhere they gathered information and became known for their low-key listening approach. Thus they built up their own and others' confidence. They engaged with people in a non-threatening way to find out about their lives and about what might be possible to do together to improve their conditions. As they showed that they respected the humanity they had in common with the people they addressed they found that they were trusted with information that enabled their project to develop. At **Mornington** there is a similar commitment to listening to what people in the neighbourhood have to say about their own lives, to respecting them and valuing them for who they are and to empowering rather than 'doing for' them. As local people felt themselves informed and part of what was happening, the Mornington project gained a reputation as a safe and accessible place and workers became familiar figures on the streets. Then in the aftermath of multiple murders in the neighbourhood, when it was natural to talk about what sustained individuals and groups through such trauma, staff and volunteers found that they were trusted enough to be invited to speak about their own values.

Knocknagoney congregation transformed their church hall into a community asset. The joint management committee offers ongoing opportunity for continued learning and trust building. The minister continues to stress the interdependence of congregation and community and, as the congregation slowly adjusts its self-perception, he has a sense of increasing local interest, ownership and trust permeating the neighbourhood. He finds one small sign of this in local children exercising their freedom to play within the grounds of the building complex with an absence of vandalism of the kind suffered by other community buildings in the area. Members of the **Ballysillan** congregation struggle to accept the need for change to a completely different way of 'being church'. They acknowledge that this will be a long-term operation that allows them no possibility of opting out of engagement with the angry and fractured community of which they are part. They recognise the limitations on what they can achieve in their volatile area of north Belfast, but are determined to 'do what they can with young people' there. **Shankill** parish could have reinforced the tendency to polarisation of the town that it sees itself existing to serve. Instead, in cooperation with all and any people of good will, it developed a new understanding and practice of itself as a community church and is pressing forward with its Jethro project. **Flax** emerged as a response to inter-community violence. Two of its founders, members of Catholic religious orders, intended that through the trust the church should find a way to engage directly with what they saw as the social and economic causes or rivalry and hatred. The resulting organisation has a greater range, scope and strength than either of them foresaw. The Catholic parish from which the **Omagh** Boys and Girls Club emerged made a gift of the site on which the new Station Centre is built. This signals a serious and lasting commitment to the social cohesion and community well being of the whole town.

In the late 1990s **YMCA** (National Council) underwent a period of intense introspection and analysis in order to identify the changes that might be required in order to pursue its mission more effectively. In 1999 a strategic review of the organisation was carried out and the resulting document was presented at a series of regional consultations throughout Ireland. The exercise focused on changes in the environment within which the movement currently operates. It identified, for example, higher expectations of young people, alternative provision in the community, new patterns of funding, issues of health and safety, the political climate and the increasing willingness of churches to become involved in community work. Questions about the movement's rationale, focus, role in the community, scope and structure were also addressed.

The National Council of YMCAs has now translated its mission into policy terms. It has formally embraced both a community relations and an anti-sectarian policy and has put in place a mechanism for measuring and evaluating their implementation. This change has significance across the whole of the island of Ireland, but its impact is more acutely felt in the north. What was previously an exclusively Protestant organisation is now set upon a path of fostering a sense of openness and inclusiveness, of exposing its members to different faith perspectives, different emphases and varying practice. This represents both a risk to the organisation and a direct challenge to some of the prejudices that are endemic in society in Northern Ireland and it is crucially dependent upon the relationships and levels of trust within YMCA (Central) and between it and the local associations.

SOCIAL CAPITAL AND RELIGIOUS VALUES

As was noted in Section 1 of this report, neighbourhood regeneration initiatives and growing interest in social capital have run together in New Labour thinking (Szreter, 2000). The PAT 17 report links church-based projects in Local Strategic Partnerships with the strengthening of social capital (Home Office, 2000). It was also observed in Section 1 that the idea of social capital presents a whole range of problems. These are to do with the theory of social capital, with its utility as an analytical tool, with its measurement and with the plasticity that allows it to be bent to a political agenda. It would be naive to imagine it as a commodity that can be spread equally across South Armagh and North Down with uniform beneficial effect. Notes in Appendix I provide some background information on these issues. For the purposes of this study and to explore how useful social capital might be as a lens through which to view faith-based voluntary activity, a broad approach to the concept has been adopted. It is that of the British Cabinet Office, namely, 'all those institutional arrangements, networks and relationships which promote understanding, trust and mutual respect; allow communities to pursue shared goals more effectively; improve information flows; and generally improve the quality of life' (Cabinet Office, 1999, p. 137). On this baggy understanding of social capital, it is clear that those values that have been identified as some of the most distinctive aspects of faith-based organisations (Cameron, 2001), relationship and mutuality, cooperation and trust, fit comfortably within it.

These values are encouraged within the faith tradition of the twelve FBOs. They call their adherents to attend to the commitments and promises that they make in relationships of mutual care and regard and to how they follow them through in daily life. One of the ways in which this call is conveyed is in the words and stories of scripture that are read aloud at times of worship. Some of the most familiar are known beyond the faith community of their origin. 'Do as you would be done by' is a popular expression of the duty to care for the neighbour (Mark 12; Kee, 1993), perhaps one of the most powerful motors of bonding social capital formation. The extension of this, the assertion that care for one's neighbour is a duty owed to God, has become universally familiar in the form of the story of the Samaritan, the outcast who took care of the half-dead stranger he met by chance (Luke 10; Kee, 1993). As a story of openness to the stranger and of generalised trust, it urges a degree of bridging social capital alongside existing bonding capital in the network of all who hear it. The ideal for that network, as it is described in scriptural terms (1 Corinthians; Kee, 1993), is one in which new people are incorporated and where all are valued regardless of role and all work together for the greater good. There are acknowledged norms of behaviour; there is authority and enforcement; gifts are recognised, shared and developed; there is capacity to grow, learn and adapt. This is a powerful evocation of bonding social capital in the way that the parable of the Samaritan provides an example of the bridging kind (Pollitt, 2000). Even a small mainstream congregation has a shared belief system that encourages social capital formation of both the bonding and bridging kind. It may also include linking social capital with professional and business networks. The shared system and language allow members to communicate their ideas and make sense of common experiences and ideas in a way that facilitates joint action.

Section 7 Discussion and Conclusions

The prayer 'your kingdom come' holds up the ideal of a society of justice and peace, carries the expression of a hope for it, and stimulates an intent to work towards it. Results from any subsequent action will not necessarily be dramatic, but they can be distinctive, as is illustrated by the neighbourhood regeneration work of the Benmoe congregation discussed below.

'Regeneration' is a word that appears in connection with neighbourhood renewal in the remits of the Policy Action Teams (Home Office, 1999 & 2000). People who live in an area considered to be in need of regeneration have heard outside 'experts' speak of the intractable problems of their community, the levels of crime, unemployment, health and educational attainment, of perceptions of what is lacking rather than of what they, the insiders, perceive it has. With negative language the only or main one in use, the community can come to see itself in terms of what is bad about its life. But regeneration is a strong theological idea that appears in the Church Urban Fund document, Flourishing Communities (Chester et al. 1999). Drawing upon its theological roots, the authors give the word a more positive ring, with references to holistic renewal and change. Physical urban decay is seen as only part of the story. The other part is, on this understanding, the lack of self-esteem, sense of meaning and purpose in life that is reinforced in individual people by being in a 'bad' community. The community worker and her volunteers from the Benmoe congregation have made a striking impact on the estate where their pastoral centre is based. Part of the reason may be that they are not outside 'experts', but people who live in the area. Another part may be that they are addressing the lack of self- esteem by fostering a sense of what is positive and possible in the neighbourhood. Underneath their policy and practice may be the deeper religious understanding of regeneration that frees them to bypass the negative professional assessment of the area and to accept and honour the reality of people's everyday lives and to speak the language of respect, affirmation and hope. That notion of hopeful regeneration is sustained in the Benmoe members, as in other congregations, through the scriptural stories of compassion and relationship that they hear and are taught regularly and repeatedly in worship and in study groups.

Recent empirical evidence from the United States indicates that it is 'in the theological teaching of most religions and on the shared and normative experience of most congregations and congregants' that activity to enhance the quality of life of others in the wider community is rooted and based (Cnaan, 1999, p. 28). This faith-related vision possessed by congregations reinforces the values behind community engagement. It turns congregations into more than providers of a context for relationship building, though they often do this. It reinforces a culture that leads to engagement with disadvantaged people, whether that engagement finds expression within the congregation or through the involvement of its people in other community settings. It makes congregations creators of social capital (Bedford, 2002), and the church 'the one institution that we might expect to build social capital' (Messer, 1998).

Findings from the United States show that FBOs can build social capital by mobilising resources that might not otherwise be mobilised to address community problems. They can raise consciousness about community problems among people who would not otherwise be aware or engaged. They can create linkages that would not normally exist between social groups. They can empower social groups that normally have little influence (Allen Hayes, 2001). The profiles above show churches and para-churches in Northern Ireland engaged in these very processes.

In all of the organisations examined in this study there is strong evidence of what Albert Hirschman says 'is best described not as labor or work, but as striving' (Hirschman, 1984, p. 91), the effect of which is to blur the edges of any cost-benefit calculus. What he describes is a social energy that transcends rational self-interest and market transactions in order to promote social cooperation. As he sees it, this investment in individual and group identity feeds into the creation of dense social networks and better economic and social outcomes. Social capital theory, according to the Putnam model, would support this kind of connection, holding that where society is characterised by a measure of trust, enjoys rich cross links, vibrant interaction and strong networks, then economic growth tends to follow.

However in faith-based organisations social networks and human relationships tend to be valued for their own intrinsic worth, more than as a means to the end of socio-economic development or civic participation. The theological roots underlying this perspective are the same as those that lead members of FBOs in one deprived locality to work for constructive change and in another to ask questions about why society is structured so as to concentrate poverty in a particular area. In **Holy Family** parish, a place that exhibits a vibrant sense of community and mutual responsibility within a bleak setting, there is what the administrator calls 'the local reflection of a global problem, the division between the haves and the have-nots within the parish boundary'.

Section 7 Discussion and Conclusions

BRINGING TOGETHER POLICY, PRACTICE AND RESEARCH

It would be unreal to claim that all churches and para-church organisations in Northern Ireland are like those profiled in this report. What is sure is that, if social capital is important, here is a vital source of it that should not continue to be overlooked by policy-makers. Even if social capital may not have quite the potency that some of its proponents suggest, two key points still stand.

The first is that the contribution of these faith-based organisations is manifestly not simply for the benefit of their members only. Therefore any definition of the voluntary sector that excludes them is deficient. The second is that the quality and range of their contribution to the health of society in Northern Ireland is significant enough to place them squarely and urgently within the public policy frame.

Whether, and if so how, the churches in Northern Ireland might be encouraged to work together systematically on local community issues within an agreed one-community strategy that would challenge sectarianism in the long term is a question that remains to be answered. In Britain the present Labour government's model of dialogue with faith communities has encouraged interesting developments. Taking the example of just one London borough, a research project carried out by the Office for Public Management resulted in a range of recommendations that included the appointment of a senior policy officer (faith communities) to open up a dialogue and win trust (Camden, 2000). Lincolnshire County Council recently advertised three community development officer posts, adding that applicants 'must be prepared to work with the local Christian community and thus a good working knowledge of the Christian Church is desirable' (*Church Times*, December 2002). The Churches Regional Commission for Yorkshire and Humber last year appointed a director and a policy officer to spearhead and develop policy for church social action. The Anglican Diocese of Leicester is currently advertising a post of regeneration development officer for the faith communities, to be underpinned by the Government Empowerment Fund (*Church Times*, 10/01/03).

The examples above show that, in Britain, the model of dialogue has brought the issue of faith-based social action and community development into fine focus, sharpened the challenge and presented unequivocal acknowledgement and affirmation of its place firmly within the voluntary sector alongside the work of other agencies in civil society. Such affirmation is lacking in Northern Ireland. As was noted in Section 1 of this report, the words of the Prime Minister to faith communities, 'we want you as partners, not substitutes', have not yet permeated this part of the UK. A recent report on church-based social action in England has a heavy resonance in Northern Ireland when it says that churches

> *have to function in an atmosphere of public scepticism, not to say suspicion, about religion in general and their motives and efficacy in the social field* (Sweeney, 2001).

There is therefore a job to done in breaking down suspicion and misunderstanding and in raising awareness of the fact that, while the central purpose of faith communities may be said to be the practice of their faith, social action is a fundamental part of the practice of most faiths because the requirement to serve people in need is part of their core teaching. A degree of hiddenness about some aspects of the work that churches do may be appropriate. Nevertheless, as organisations operating in the public realm, it might be considered to be in the interests of everyone that their contribution to society be more transparent and widely known. There is a need to bring together policy, practice and research in the way that the Church of Scotland is doing (Flint, 2001) and the Churches Community Work Alliance (CCWA) is seeking to do in Northern Ireland on behalf of all the main churches. CCWA is a formal network of Churches Together in Britain and Ireland (CTBI) that collaborates with many voluntary organisations and fosters, develops and supports good community work practice by churches. Such a body, with links both to government and to all of the churches, could play a vital role in providing information, advice and training for church leaders at central and at local level. It could also cover the traditional role of the umbrella organisation as lobbying, representative and network organisation. In view of the lack of baseline information, the magnitude of the task of social transformation in Northern Ireland and the potential gains to society as a whole from its work, such an agency should have research muscle and capacity for provision of a full range of professional, advisory and technical services to support developmental projects as well as to encourage start ups.

There is experience from elsewhere to build upon. Making due allowances for cultural differences, there may be something to be learned from the way in which the US Senate's working group has gone about tackling issues of great complexity in the area of human needs and faith-based and community initiatives (Finding Common Ground, 2002). Britain already has the advantage of the Local

Government Association's best practice guide (LGA, 2002), the DETR/Shaftesbury practitioner handbooks (Randolph-Horn, 2000) and the CCWA/CUF booklet (Finneron et al., 2001) amongst other useful publications. Northern Ireland versions of such documents could inform and stimulate debate leading to action in local communities here.

Tailored to the local needs and circumstances and featuring examples of good practice with which people from across the province could identify, such resources and tools for learning could be widely distributed to District Councils and within the churches from central authorities to local church forums (where they exist). This would:

- raise the profile and highlight the potential of faith-based action to target social need;
- draw attention to the changing face of local government and the opportunities for partnerships;
- stimulate reflexivity and discussion on what might be undertaken by churches together;
- nurture cross-fertilisation amongst varying perspectives and approaches;
- encourage shared and broad based action that avoided duplication of effort.

The umbrella body could also back up the distribution of such resources with a range of workshops for practitioners, on-site training events and mentoring in community development work run by peripatetic staff or others with experience and expertise in the field.

SOME RECOMMENDATIONS

To churches

- Churches have enormous theological resources to shape a social vision that would enhance the reach of current government policy. They should take confidence in this fact and, from a position of cooperation with sister churches, collaboration with public and statutory bodies and solidarity with socially excluded people, they should actively look for ways to contribute to the making of social policy.

- Churches should examine their theological resources and open themselves to a renewed understanding of their embeddedness in local communities and of their acts of public worship as socially significant expressions of inclusion and social capital formation.

- Churches have trained leaders who are often people of vision and commitment. They should review their programmes of training and consider including modules that build upon their leaders' strengths to promote an enabling and facilitating approach to ministry. The United Reformed Church module on church-related community work for its ministers provides one example of good practice.

- Churches have large human capital resources. They should more actively and systematically encourage their people to see the volunteering of their time, energy and expertise to the well being of the local community as a vital expression of faith.

- Churches possess significant physical resources in terms of buildings in key locations. They should look again at the totality of the resources represented by their faith, their people and their premises and seek ways of using them to build community morale, cooperation and confidence.

- Churches know the value of networks. They should more wholeheartedly grasp the opportunities that are available to them within voluntary sector networks of communication and support and should further benefit their local communities through the use of the bridging and linking social capital from their wider contacts.

- Churches could become more sensitive to the limited effectiveness of working in isolation and should add value to their social action by collaborating with other agencies in the work of building social cohesion and developing stable local communities.

- Churches can create encounters between people who would otherwise never meet, crossing divisions of gender, age and class. They should build into their local strategy a community project dimension that would give practical expression to this inclusive dimension to their faith. This might take service provision form or, for example, an exercise to monitor the impact of specific social policies upon socially excluded groups in the neighbourhood.

Section 7 Discussion and Conclusions   159

- Churches should become more aware of the importance of research and evaluation for the provision of ready examples of good practice. These examples could be widely shared in a way that would both encourage the mission of the churches and command the attention of policy-makers and inform their decisions.

- Churches should do more to raise the public profile of the nature, range and scale of their deep-rooted commitment to the wellbeing of society in Northern Ireland and should combat public ignorance of their activities or misconceptions about their purposes that are rooted in historical legacy.

- Churches should develop closer contacts with local authorities, support their attempts to serve all of the people within their boundaries and commit to partnerships in local regeneration initiatives.

- Churches should more enthusiastically exploit the opportunities offered by church forums, where they exist, as means of bringing together diverse people and outlooks, for dissemination of information and as instruments of united action.

- Churches should support and benefit from the skills and expertise of an existing umbrella body like the Churches Community Work Alliance for training and for information about practice and about funding streams.

To policy-makers

- Policy-makers appear to have a limited perception of churches and other faith-based organisations. They should invest energy, resources and time in uncovering how these bodies encounter and minister to people in the context of their whole life experience, offering different types of social capital that are important at different times over an individual's lifetime. They should also make themselves aware of the work of such bodies towards transformation and regeneration at many levels from the spiritual to the political.

- Policy-makers should seek out and renew the channels of communication with the churches and fully appraise them, at local as well as central level, of the thrust and direction of contemporary policy. They should invite the participation of the churches in meeting policy objectives that are in line with their mission and in a way that encourages them to share information, understand and support each other and work together.

- Bearing in mind the way in which churches already cooperate with local authorities elsewhere in the UK and recognising the signs of a growing willingness to work collaboratively in Northern Ireland, policy-makers should facilitate the participation of churches by enabling the production and widespread dissemination of Northern Ireland versions of training and information publications already in use in Britain. The DETR and LGA manuals provide good examples (Randolph-Horn, 2000; LGA, 2002).

- Policy-makers should take steps to ensure that orientation and awareness training opportunities are put in place for government officers engaging with churches and, where these do not exist, consider appointing liaison or development officers to facilitate the process of dialogue and discovery.

- Policy-makers should provide clear information about funding streams and, with appropriate safeguards, make such funding more readily accessible.

APPENDIX I NOTES ON SOCIAL CAPITAL

This section is included in order to provide a glimpse of the complexity that comes with the concept of social capital, one that is not always acknowledged by those who employ the term. Three dimensions to this complexity are relevant to the project report. The purpose here is not to enter into the debate that surrounds each of these dimensions, nor indeed to offer a treatment of the contribution of the seminal thinkers, but to alert the reader to the ideological argument about social capital and to mark the fact that it is controversial also in terms of definition and measurement.

IDEOLOGICAL DEBATE

Where (after Putnam) social capital is commonly taken to indicate the strength and wealth of local associations and where it is promoted as at least part of the answer to a problem such as social exclusion in society, there is the danger that the reality of the significance of power and local class relations may be missed and that existing power relations may be reinforced. Critics of the language of social capital say it can appear to depoliticise the issues around poverty and social justice when it accentuates the importance of voluntary associations in civic engagement. Such associations, far from being necessarily democratically representative or accountable, can be used to further the interests of powerful individuals or groups in society while bypassing time consuming contestational politics. It has been observed that the voluntary activities of some of these organisations may suit the agenda of a government that wants, for example, to make substantive cuts in public expenditure. Indeed they may contribute to the development of a culture that breeds an expectation that disadvantaged people should get together to pull themselves out of their own predicament.

This project report demonstrates that churches have their own theological 'take' on social capital. Further, they may be expected to know both the difference between their own mission and the instrumental designs on them by government and where the two overlap. Certainly they have been at times amongst the strongest critics of the thrust of government social policy and, if the survey findings in this report are reliable, they are unlikely to be proponents of the view that the poor can fend for themselves. This aspect of the debate, namely how the concept has been put to use, is an important one and writers like Theda Skocpol

(1996), Bob Foley and Mike Edwards (1998), Richard Couto (1999), Ben Fine (2001) and John Harriss (2002) offer pathways to an understanding of social capital that is less mainstream but nonetheless not to be ignored. This brings us to the matter of definition.

DEFINITION

The idea that social relationships constitute a resource is an old one. The first reference to social capital is generally reckoned to be in a piece of writing on the importance of community participation in enhancing school performance. This is the world of 1916, but we can still get a good sense of the idea of a resource and of the broad intuitive appeal that it carries.

> *In the use of the phrase 'social capital' ... We do not refer to real estate or to personal property or cash, but rather to that in life which tends to make those tangible substances (that) count for most in the daily lives of people: namely good will, fellowship, sympathy, and social intercourse among the individuals and families who make up a social unit. ... If (an individual comes) into contact with his neighbor, and they with other neighbors, there will be an accumulation of social capital, which may immediately satisfy his social needs and which may bear a social potentiality sufficient to the substantial improvement of living conditions in the whole community* (Hanifan, 1916 p. 130).

More recently the concept featured in the cultural theory of Pierre Bourdieu and the sociology of James Coleman, both regarded as principal theoreticians of social capital. But it was in the 1990s, largely through the influence of the work of Robert Putnam, that social capital was shaped to occupy its position as the ingredient increasingly seen as critical for good governance and, if the World Bank economists were to be believed, for economic development. Before turning to Putnam, it is important to recall the independent and contrasting approaches to the concept of social capital that were emerging in the 1980s in the work of Coleman and Bourdieu.

Appendix 1 Notes on Social Capital

Pierre Bourdieu

Writing from within the European sociological tradition in the 1960s and 70s, Pierre Bourdieu was interested in issues of power and position in society, the relations between groups and classes and their access to resources. He saw social capital as just one of 'three fundamental species' of capital that have to be considered together, the others being economic and cultural. He defined social capital as 'the aggregate of the actual or potential resources which are linked to possession of a durable network of more or less institutionalized relationships of mutual acquaintance and recognition ... which provides each of its members with the backing of collectively owned capital' (Bourdieu, 1997).

Bourdieu focused on how individuals benefit themselves and each other through relationships deliberately created with this in mind. The idea is of a process by which the group or class reproduces its way of life and position through maintaining closed networks of people who share the same cultural habits and economic resources. This is a view of social capital not as the possession of society as a whole, but rather as an aspect of the differentiation of classes and an instrument of power. More about the implications of this view will be offered when we look at measurement below.

James Coleman

James Coleman, as an American sociologist and rational choice theorist, gave close attention to individual and social action. His formulation of the idea of social capital reflects this theoretical position. He defined social capital as 'a particular kind of resource available to an actor', comprising a 'variety of different entities having two characteristics in common: they all consist of some aspect of social structure, and they facilitate certain actions of the individuals who are within the structure'. He continued. 'Unlike other forms of capital, social capital inheres in the structures between persons and among persons. It is lodged neither in individuals nor in physical implements of production' (Coleman, 1990, p. 302).

Coleman provided examples to show how reciprocity and trust in social relations are of value. They help reduce transaction costs, they facilitate communication of information and they provide a kind of insurance located within mutual obligations. His use of examples itself showed how context-specific the value of this social capital actually is.

Robert Putnam

With the work of Robert Putnam, an American political scientist, the concept of social capital attracted international attention. Putnam drew on his research on regional government in Italy, applied its findings to levels of civic engagement in the United States and helped promote his ideas on social capital globally. Where Bourdieu and Coleman saw the promise of social capital for individuals and groups in community, Putnam developed its promise in terms of the ability to mobilise resources in support of community or country. For him it could be a property of a whole society.

Building on de Tocqueville's enthusiasm for voluntary associations as the roots of the stability of America's democratic government, Putnam gives great significance to the place and density of these organisations in society and to participatory behaviour in a community, seeing them as a source of social capital of a relentlessly positive and celebratory kind. His reference to the role of bowling clubs in 1950s America as not just providers of recreation but sustainers of the wider social fabric has both caught the popular imagination and given social capital the aura of a public good with accompanying policy relevance and appeal. Indeed his thought has become so influential that social capital is often read as shorthand for the vitality of civic life. His definition is deceptively succinct: 'features of social life - networks, norms, and trust - that enable participants to act together more effectively to pursue shared objectives' (Putnam, 1996). Although Putnam himself disavowed the view that government can be replaced by civil society, this is the understanding of social capital that has been taken up by those who believe that government policies should have more to do with facilitating the development of self-help in deprived communities than with redistribution of resources that might help build the capacity of local organisations and stiffen the sinews of political and economic development.

Jo Anne Schneider

Jo Anne Schneider features here for several reasons. One is that she takes contemporary American faith-based organisations as the context for her serious empirical exploration of the concept. Another is that she pursues an independent line of thought, building upon the neglected Bourdieu as well as upon Coleman to create a finely focused way of looking at how social capital forms and operates. Yet another has to do with the way in which her weighing of the exclusive dimension of social capital speaks to the sectarian condition of churches in

Appendix 1 Notes on Social Capital 165

Northern Ireland.

With economic capital understood as money required for an activity, human capital understood as education and skills needed to fulfil a goal and cultural capital understood as knowing how to act and present oneself in order to fit in, Schneider sees social capital as providing the way in to these other kinds of mutually interdependent and re-enforcing capital. For her the concept is 'a metaphor for a process that enables people to gain access to the material resources of a community'. It refers to social relationships and patterns of trust that enable people to gain access to resources like government services or jobs. It refers also to social relationships that help organisations find funding, volunteers, employees, information, programme participants and other things they need to survive.

As can be seen from her Kenosha study, Schneider underpins this view with social science formulations of the concept in which social capital is actually a mechanism for exclusion and often 'the means through which a small group shares its resources among defined members' (Schneider, 2001).

This 'process', 'mechanism' or 'means' requires two elements. The first is 'relationships based in enforceable trust with people or organisations who have access to resources needed to meet basic necessities and fulfill goals'. The second is 'knowledge of cultural cues which indicate that an individual is a member of a group and should be given access to those relationships'. The first dimension includes connections, trust and networks with appropriate information. The second refers to access to cultural capital essential to use these social networks. From this approach it can be clearly seen how social capital and cultural capital, though separate concepts, work together to help people attain their goals. It also becomes clearer that with social capital embedded in social, cultural and institutional environments where power, information and networks are unevenly distributed, not everyone has the same access to it.

MEASUREMENT

When this project began, a scan of the available literature indicated that instruments for the measurement of social capital were under continuing development. This is unsurprising given the variety of approaches to the term reflected in the brief remarks above. The lack of consensus on definition presented difficulty for measurement and for the design of questionnaires purporting to capture elements of social capital.

This can be illustrated quite simply by looking again at Bourdieu and Coleman and isolating a difference in their understanding of the concept. Each of these thinkers focused on social ties that make resources or opportunities available to individuals. Bourdieu broke social capital into two elements, namely the social relationship itself and the resources to which it could enable access. Coleman concentrated not on the resources as such, but on the social processes allowing individuals to draw upon them. The way in which these social processes develop was understood differently by the two theorists. For Bourdieu they were constrained by underlying structural economic organisation. For Coleman they resulted from the free choice of individuals to build networks to further their self-interest.

The point of relevance here for questionnaires setting out to measure social capital is this. Measurement of social capital as understood by Bourdieu involves a grasp of the material conditions affecting social process. In the Coleman framework measurement entails a consideration of motivation. This is where Putnam picked up and extended the concept to describe a more general measure of social trust and social inclusion across a whole society. In his analysis of differences in democracy and economic development in regions of Italy he focused on the creation of civic norms that he saw as leading to the socioeconomic order. Bourdieu's argument would run precisely the other way round.

In the light of this it is an unremarkable thought that different understandings of social capital lead to different measures. However it was less obvious at the beginning of this project as the researcher grappled with the literature both fuelling and fuelled by a debate spanning disciplinary, cultural and geographical boundaries.

From 1996 through to 2001 the World Bank Social Capital Initiative engaged in a sustained effort to bring rigour and clarity to the task of measurement. A synthesis of its findings and recommendations came out in recent months (Grootaert and Van Bastelaer, 2002). In keeping with Putnam's line of thinking, modules were added to existing social surveys like the World Values Survey in order to identify such components of social capital as trust, civic participation, social engagement or reciprocity. There was a growing awareness that the concept encapsulated something important, but its contours were shadowy and there was no generic

Appendix 1 Notes on Social Capital 167

format for an indicator of its presence, quality or strength. In Britain a social capital module was in development for the General Household Survey, but the National Statistics Social Capital Question Bank had not yet come on line (National Statistics Online, 2001).

A way through the reigning complexity was presented by an Australian study that was attractive because of its ground-up quality (Onyx and Bullen, 1997). Onyx and Bullen started off with basic questions and proceeded to a careful exploration of the concept of social capital from both a theoretical and an empirical basis. They identified three main factors as of particular importance, community participation, proactivity and trust. They isolated eight distinct elements as defining social capital. Some of the questions built around these factors and elements seemed to offer explanatory potential in the Northern Ireland context and where they overlapped the World Values Survey approach they were adapted for the project questionnaire. In addition, questions from instruments already developed for surveying religious attitudes in Northern Ireland were also incorporated in an attempt to avoid some of the insensitivities in this area (Boal et al., 1997).

Forrest and Kearns' work on social capital and social cohesion became available too late for the questionnaire design, but their ideas on eight social capital domains echoed the notion of eight social capital elements in the Australian study. Their work was useful for the categorisation of some of the project findings.

Also just too late to be of use to the project, work on the evaluation of publicly funded community based and voluntary activity in Northern Ireland issued in an interim report (Morrissey and McGinn, 2001). The authors drew upon the indicators of social capital identified in empirical research under the World Bank initiative. In particular they turned to the attempt by Krishna and Shrader (1999) to devise a uniform method of measurement in the belief that, whatever the context or conceptual approach, a fairly constant basic list of categories under which to examine social capital will apply. Presenting four levels at which social capital may be said to operate (individual and household; organisational, neighbourhood and community; regional and national), Morrissey and McGinn offered a number of criteria by which to decide if social capital formation is taking place at each level. They identified indicators that they believe to be most relevant for the Northern Ireland voluntary sector. Their work shows significant investigative promise.

APPENDIX II RATIONALE FOR THE AMENDED PROJECT DESIGN

The project design was amended as follows. The original design envisaged two separate questionnaires, one on voluntary activity (A) and one on social capital (B), being administered to three respondents in each organisation. This would have brought an optimal return of 72. In fact these two questionnaires were combined into one and distributed to ten respondents in each organisation, allowing an optimal return of 120.

For the reasons advanced below, changes were also made to the nature and number of interviews conducted. Instead of 36 by telephone and 25 face-to-face as in the original design, a total of 46 face-to-face interviews was conducted (3 each for 7 profiles and 5 each for 5 case studies).

THE QUESTIONNAIRE

The need for an adjustment to the design of the survey became clear once the process of drafting the questionnaires for piloting got under way in Phase 1. It seemed, on reflection, simpler and more practical both to combine questionnaires A and B into one and to make greater use of them. Each organisation received 10 instead of 3 questionnaires, making for an optimal return of 120. This promised to strengthen this phase of the analysis. It did not however alleviate the difficulties facing any attempt to get an empirical grip on social capital (See Appendix I above).

The temptation to generate information that was interesting but not strictly necessary to the project proved too great to resist. The task of responding to a list of eighty questions is perhaps a daunting one. The task of analysis has been correspondingly complex and time consuming. There were two other significant flaws in the questionnaire. Though an attempt was made to avoid such an obvious danger, in the event the survey instrument was more Protestant than Catholic in flavour, a fact that would have emerged had it been piloted in both settings. Also the link between the interview schedule and the questionnaire could have been stronger. In the event the questionnaire was not sent out with a covering letter, as had originally been intended, but was introduced at the interview with the leader of each organisation. This allowed acknowledgment of the bias in the

Appendix II Rationale For The Amended Project Design

questionnaire and opened discussion of the need to ensure a balance of respondents. This went some way towards ensuring that the response rate was not lower than it turned out to be.

INTERVIEWS

Once the outer parameters of the study had been established along with a list of possible churches and faith-based organisations for study, it became necessary to decide which FBOs to approach in order to find out more directly about their operations. Then came the decision about which to seek to include in the study, followed by the process of negotiating access and of gaining the cooperation of the leaders. When an introductory letter had been drafted and background material prepared, further practical questions arose. In negotiating access, was the mailing to be sent cold, or was a telephone introduction to be effected beforehand? If so, how was that introductory conversation to relate to the proposed telephone interview? The approach adopted was to telephone first. In some instances it was necessary to speak more than once before arriving at an understanding that a preliminary interview might take place, that it would involve no further obligation and that any agreement to include the FBO in the study would follow only after further consideration on both sides.

In the course of these tentative conversations it became clear that the proposed semi-structured interviews would be more satisfactorily conducted face-to-face. This had both time and cost implications. It also meant that travelling distance became an issue narrowing the final choice of locations beyond Belfast. There were potential gains to the project in terms of 'feel' for, and insight into, each organisation, for the quality of the relationship between people on the ground and the researcher, for the integrity of the eventual decision over case studies and for the value of the dissemination event. The argument for a change of method was irresistible.

APPENDIX III *THE SEMI-STRUCTURED INTERVIEW SCHEDULE*

1. Basic information: - type and name of organisation; denomination or network; date of foundation; size/membership; name/address/telephone number of contact person; position/role in organisation.

2. I would like to hear something of the story of this organisation, where it fits in to the local community and how it came to be where it is today ..

3. Can you say a little about what it sets out to do and whether its objectives are expressed in a mission statement?

4. Can you give me a picture of the range of its activities?

5. Tell me about your buildings, how and by whom they are used ..

6. Who participates in your programmes .. numbers of staff and use of volunteers .. where do they come from?

7. Would you say that there is a reasonable level of local ownership of what goes on in the organisation?

8. How would you describe the main benefits of the organisation's activities?

9. How does the organisation decide what its programme of activities will be and who makes the important decisions?

10. What are the pressing issues for the organisation at present?

11. What does your own role involve .. and what are you most important relationships?

12. Has funding for your activities been a difficulty.. where has it come from in the main?

13. Have formal research methods been of use in helping your organisation understand itself and its place in the local community?

Appendix III The Semi-Structured Interview Schedule   171

14. What links do you have with other churches .. other organisations and agencies with an interest in the area .. and why?

15. Are you working in a formal partnership with any other body?

16. Is there a cross-community dimension to your activities?

17. Where does the faith dimension come into it all?

18. What changes have you seen and how have they been handled by leadership and by staff/members?

19. In what way would you like to see the local neighbourhood change?

20. What is the most important aspect of the work going on here?

21. What are the elements that limit its effectiveness?

22. Where is the organisation headed?

23. Any other points to note.

APPENDIX IV *THE SURVEY QUESTIONNAIRE*

Your personal details
---

1. Are you male or female? *(Please tick)* ☐ Male   ☐ Female

2. Is your marital status ……..? *(Please tick one box)*

    ☐ Single and never married   ☐ Married

    ☐ Single by divorce, separation or annulment   ☐ Widowed

3. Do you have children? *(Please tick)* ☐ Yes   ☐ No

    If yes, how many? *(Please tick one box)*

    ☐ 1   ☐ 2   ☐ 3   ☐ 4   ☐ 5+

4. What age are you? *(Please tick one box)*

    17 & under   18-24   25-34   35-44   45-54   55-64   65 & over
    ☐   ☐   ☐   ☐   ☐   ☐   ☐

5. Is your home ……..? *(Please tick one box)*

    ☐ Rented from the Housing Executive   ☐ Owner occupied   ☐ Other

6. What type of school/college did you last attend full time? *(Please tick one box)*

    ☐ Primary/Elementary   ☐ F.E. College/Technical College

    ☐ Secondary/Intermediate   ☐ University/Poly/College of Education

    ☐ Grammar   ☐ Other *(Please specify)* …………..

Appendix IV The Survey Questionnaire 173

7. What was the home background in which you were brought up?
   (Please tick one box)

   ☐ Professional   ☐ Semi-skilled Manual

   ☐ Managerial   ☐ Unskilled Manual

   ☐ Skilled Manual   ☐ Other (Please specify)

   ☐ Clerical/Sales   .. ..

8. What is your present home background? *(Please tick one box)*

   ☐ Professional   ☐ Semi-skilled Manual

   ☐ Managerial   ☐ Unskilled Manual

   ☐ Skilled Manual   ☐ Other (Please specify)

   ☐ Clerical/Sales   .. ..

9. Have you ever been employed? *(Please tick)*   ☐ Yes   ☐ No

10. At present, are you .. .. ..? *(Please tick one box)*

    ☐ Employed full time   ☐ Student/Pupil

    ☐ Employed part time   ☐ Permanently sick/Disabled

    ☐ Unemployed less than 1 year   ☐ Training programme

    ☐ Unemployed more than 1 year   ☐ Retired

    ☐ Looking after home/family   ☐ Other

| **You, your church/FBO and community involvement** |

11. What describes your status in this church/FBO? *(Please tick one box)*

   ☐ Leader (paid)   ☐ Leader (unpaid)

   ☐ Member   ☐ Regular attender but not a member

   ☐ Occasional attender   ☐ Visitor

   ☐ Other e.g. employee

12. How did you first get involved in this church/FBO? *(Please tick one box)*

   ☐ Friend   ☐ Church evangelistic programme

   ☐ Family member   ☐ Saw the church/FBO building and visited

   ☐ Church social ministry   ☐ Saw advertisement

   ☐ FBO or leader's reputation (describe) .. ..

   ☐ Other (describe) .. ..

13. About how often in the past year have you spent time participating in each of the following activities? *(Please tick all that apply)*

	Weekly or more	Once or twice a month	A few times a year	Never	Tick if you were a leader
a. Worship services/Mass	☐	☐	☐	☐	☐
b. Teaching groups/Sunday school	☐	☐	☐	☐	☐
c. Bible/scripture study	☐	☐	☐	☐	☐
d. Work with young people	☐	☐	☐	☐	☐
e. Meetings with the leader/minister	☐	☐	☐	☐	☐

Appendix IV The Survey Questionnaire 175

f. Church/FBO committees or boards	☐	☐	☐	☐	☐
g. Community organising/development work	☐	☐	☐	☐	☐
h. Volunteer work outside the church/FBO	☐	☐	☐	☐	☐
i. Other civic and community groups	☐	☐	☐	☐	☐

14. If you do not spend much time with any of the activities listed in the last question, what are your reasons? *(Please tick all that apply)*

    ☐ I'm too busy with work, family and activities outside the church/FBO
    ☐ I'm already involved with other ministries and activities
    ☐ No one asked me to get involved
    ☐ I live too far away
    ☐ These activities are not well organised
    ☐ These activities do not seem important
    ☐ I was involved in the past and got burned out
    ☐ I don't think I'm gifted or called in this area
    ☐ Other

15. Has your church/FBO involvement increased, decreased, or stayed about the same in the last few years? *(Please tick one box)*

    ☐ Increased   ☐ Decreased   ☐ Stayed about the same

16. Do you attend religious services in the neighbourhood/parish in which you live or do you travel outside it to worship? *(Please tick one box)*

    ☐ Local neighbourhood/parish   ☐ Travel outside to worship

17. Have you ever received training sponsored by your church/FBO in the following areas? *(Please tick all that apply)*

    ☐ Lay leadership (for example, how to lead a study group)
    ☐ Evangelism
    ☐ Community or economic development ministries
    ☐ Reconciliation or cross community work

18. How often have you done any of the following over the past year for anyone outside your church/FBO membership? *(Please tick one box in each line)*

	Often	Some times	Rarely	Never
a. Talked about your religious beliefs with someone who does not share your faith	❏	❏	❏	❏
b. Given someone religious literature	❏	❏	❏	❏
c. Invited or brought someone to church for their first visit	❏	❏	❏	❏
d. Tried to make friends with someone who does not share your faith	❏	❏	❏	❏
e. Studied scripture with someone who did not know it well	❏	❏	❏	❏
f. Helped lead someone to faith	❏	❏	❏	❏
g. Provided someone in need with food, clothing or money	❏	❏	❏	❏
h. Helped someone find a job	❏	❏	❏	❏
i. Cared for someone who was sick or handicapped	❏	❏	❏	❏
j. Volunteered to provide transport or childcare	❏	❏	❏	❏
k. Counselled, comforted, prayed for or with someone facing a difficult situation	❏	❏	❏	❏
l. Provided someone with emergency housing	❏	❏	❏	❏

Appendix IV The Survey Questionnaire 177

19. Why did you do such things? *(For each of the following reasons, please circle a number between 1 and 4 showing how important it is for your involvement)*

Reason	Extremely important ...			...Not at all important
a. Showing compassion to people in need	1	2	3	4
b. Helping to make society more just	1	2	3	4
c. Experiencing God in a deeper way	1	2	3	4
d. Bringing people served by the church/FBO's service and outreach to faith	1	2	3	4
e. Bringing people served by the church/FBO's service and outreach to your church/FBO as potential members	1	2	3	4
f. Obeying a sense of call or direction from God	1	2	3	4
g. Showing thanks for what God has done for you	1	2	3	4
h. Doing what is expected by church/FBO leaders	1	2	3	4

Your particular church/FBO

20. Below is a list of words or phrases that might be used to describe a church/FBO. *(Please circle a number from 1 to 4 to indicate how you think each describes yours)*

	Very much describes this church			Does not at all describe this church
a. Traditional	1	2	3	4
b. Like a family	1	2	3	4
c. Social agent for change	1	2	3	4
d. Refuge for members	1	2	3	4

e. Evangelistic	1	2	3	4
f. Empowering	1	2	3	4
g. Respected by others	1	2	3	4
h. Compassionate	1	2	3	4
i. Community partner	1	2	3	4

21. Does your church/FBO have a mission statement or a vision statement? *(Please tick one box)*
  ☐ Yes ☐ No ☐ Not sure

22. Do you have a sense of belonging to this church/FBO? *(Please tick one box)*

    ☐ Yes, a strong sense of belonging   ☐ No, but I am a new member/attender

    ☐ Yes, yet not as strongly as in the past   ☐ No, and I wish I did by now

    ☐ Yes, a growing sense of belonging   ☐ No, but I'm happy to stay on the fringe

23. Below are eight things that many church/FBO leaders do. What kinds of ministry do you consider most and least important for them to do? *(Please tick one box in each line)*

	Most Important	Somewhat Important	Least Important	Not Sure
a. Co-ordinate social ministry programmes	☐	☐	☐	☐
b. Counsel people with personal, family and/or work related problems	☐	☐	☐	☐
c. Bring new people to faith	☐	☐	☐	☐
d. Address social justice issues and work toward political change	☐	☐	☐	☐

Appendix IV The Survey Questionnaire

		Excellent	Good	Fair	Poor
e.	Help people grow spiritually	❏	❏	❏	❏
f.	Apply scripture to modern day issues	❏	❏	❏	❏
g.	Visit the sick, shut-in and grieving	❏	❏	❏	❏
h.	Celebrate the sacraments/ordinances of the church	❏	❏	❏	❏

24. How would you rate how your church/FBO deals with the following organisational issues? *(Please tick one box in each line)*

		Excellent	Good	Fair	Poor	Not Sure
a.	Keeping people informed about the various groups and ministry opportunities	❏	❏	❏	❏	❏
b.	Giving people opportunities to make input into decisions affecting the church/FBO	❏	❏	❏	❏	❏
c.	Dealing with disagreement and conflict	❏	❏	❏	❏	❏

25. Would you describe your church/FBO as a spiritually vital and alive community? *(Please tick one box)*

   ❏ Yes, definitely; this church/FBO is spiritually alive and growing

   ❏ Yes, somewhat; the church/FBO is moving toward greater spiritual vitality

   ❏ Mixed; some are very spiritually alive, others do not care about spiritual things

   ❏ No, not really; this church/FBO is not focused on spiritual life or growth

   ❏ Not sure

26. Please tick a box in each line to indicate how satisfactory you think work is in the following areas of ministry activity in your church/FBO. *(If you think a particular activity does not apply to your situation, please leave boxes in that line blank)*

		Very Satisfactory	Somewhat Satisfactory	Somewhat Unsatisfactory	Very Unsatisfactory	Not Sure
a.	Providing aid and social services for people in need in the community	☐	☐	☐	☐	☐
b.	Assisting neighbourhood and/or community development	☐	☐	☐	☐	☐
c.	Welcoming people of all and every background into the church/FBO	☐	☐	☐	☐	☐
d.	Organising groups to change society or influence politics	☐	☐	☐	☐	☐
e.	Taking the Gospel into the community	☐	☐	☐	☐	☐
f.	Providing a caring ministry to people who are sick, shut in, or in crisis	☐	☐	☐	☐	☐
g.	Training people for evangelism	☐	☐	☐	☐	☐
h.	Helping to deepen and guide the spiritual life of church attenders	☐	☐	☐	☐	☐
i.	Helping people who have dropped out of church life return to active faith	☐	☐	☐	☐	☐
j.	Working with young people to help them develop values and life skills	☐	☐	☐	☐	☐
k.	Educating the church on local area problems and social issues	☐	☐	☐	☐	☐
l.	Encouraging people to minister to others in their daily lives	☐	☐	☐	☐	☐
m.	Organising revivals and crusades that invite people to salvation	☐	☐	☐	☐	☐
n.	Training people to lead ministries	☐	☐	☐	☐	☐

Appendix IV The Survey Questionnaire

27. Please tick the one box which indicates where, in general, your church/FBO currently places a higher priority

    ☐ Social ministries

    ☐ Evangelism

    ☐ Gives about equal priority to both

28. Please tick the one box which indicates where, in general, your church/FBO currently places a higher priority

    ☐ The care and nurture of members and regular attenders

    ☐ Outreach and ministry to people who do not attend church

    ☐ Gives about equal priority to both

29. Thinking about your church/FBO's efforts to make an impact upon local social and economic life, how would you describe the overall effect of these ministries? *(Please tick one box)*

    ☐ Very significant

    ☐ Somewhat significant

    ☐ Somewhat insignificant

    ☐ Very insignificant

    ☐ Not sure

30. Thinking about your church/FBO's evangelistic activities, how would you describe their overall impact? *(Please tick one box)*

    ☐ Very significant

    ☐ Somewhat significant

    ☐ Somewhat insignificant

    ☐ Very insignificant

    ☐ Not sure

Your beliefs and opinions

31. For each set of statements listed below, please circle the number which best fits with your beliefs.

If you agree most with this statement, circle 1 or 2	*If you agree with both, circle 3*	*If you agree most with this statement, circle 4 or 5*

a. The task of the church is to work to change society   1 2 3 4 5   The task of the church is to work to change the lives of individuals

b. The way to share God's love with people is to tell them about Jesus   1 2 3 4 5   The way to share God's love with people is to demonstrate it with caring actions

c. Government is responsible for meeting the needs of the poor   1 2 3 4 5   The church is responsible for meeting the needs of the poor

d. Society is so full of sins that we can't expect it to improve much   1 2 3 4 5   Our actions can create a much better society than now exists

e. The church should focus on helping people here and now   1 2 3 4 5   The church should focus on preparing people for eternal life after death

f. Churches should care for people's social and emotional well-being — the quality of their health, economic condition, family life ...   1 2 3 4 5   Churches should care for people's spiritual well-being - the quality of their relationship with God ...

g. Poverty is largely due to a person's foolish choices or immoral lifestyle, such as laziness or drugs   1 2 3 4 5   Poverty is largely due to social, economic and political factors such as racism and lack of good job opportunities

Appendix IV The Survey Questionnaire 183

32. What do poor people need most to escape poverty? *(Please tick three boxes to indicate the things you think would help a poor person most)*

    ☐ Spiritual conversion - faith in God   ☐ A caring church family

    ☐ A good education and a decent job   ☐ A more just society

    ☐ To be treated with dignity and respect   ☐ Better personal morals or lifestyle

    ☐ Adequate government support   ☐ Other

33. How strongly do you agree or disagree with the following statements? *(Please tick one box in each line)*

		Strongly Agree	Agree	Disagree	Strongly Disagree	Not Sure
a.	The words of the Bible are to be taken literally as the word of God	☐	☐	☐	☐	☐
b.	There is a spiritual reality beyond what we can see or feel	☐	☐	☐	☐	☐
c.	Salvation comes only through Jesus Christ	☐	☐	☐	☐	☐
d.	The Holy Spirit is important to me in my daily life	☐	☐	☐	☐	☐
e.	I feel I am close to God and growing spiritually	☐	☐	☐	☐	☐

34. When you consider the qualities of a good life, how important do you think it is for people of faith to do each of the following?
    (Please tick one box in each line)

		Essential	Very Important	Somewhat Important	Not at all Important
a.	Spend time in prayer and Bible reading	☐	☐	☐	☐

	Essential	Very Important	Somewhat Important	Not at all Important
b. Actively seek social and economic justice	☐	☐	☐	☐
c. Take care of those who are sick or needy	☐	☐	☐	☐
d. Attend church regularly	☐	☐	☐	☐
e. Avoid worldly sins and temptations	☐	☐	☐	☐
f. Seek to bring others to faith	☐	☐	☐	☐
g. Practise religious values at home and at work	☐	☐	☐	☐
h. Maintain loving and stable family relationships	☐	☐	☐	☐
i. Be a good citizen and member of the community	☐	☐	☐	☐

You and your local neighbourhood

35. Were you brought up in a Protestant, Catholic or mixed area of Northern Ireland? *(Please tick one box)*

    Protestant ☐   Mixed ☐   Catholic ☐   Not brought up in N.I. ☐

36. How would you describe your neighbourhood now? *(Please tick one box)*

    ☐ All Protestant

    ☐ Mostly Protestant

    ☐ About equal numbers of Catholics and Protestants

    ☐ Mostly Catholic

    ☐ All Catholic

Appendix IV The Survey Questionnaire

37. What has happened to your neighbourhood over the last five years?
    (Please tick one box)
    ☐ It has become much more Protestant
    ☐ It has become a little more Protestant
    ☐ It has stayed about the same
    ☐ It has become a little more Catholic
    ☐ It has become much more Catholic

38. What kind of neighbourhood would you prefer to live in now?
    (Please tick one box)
    ☐ All Protestant
    ☐ Mostly Protestant
    ☐ About equal number of Protestants and Catholics
    ☐ Mostly Catholic
    ☐ All Catholic

39. Have you ever had to move house because of intimidation? *(Please tick)*
    ☐ Yes   ☐ No

40. Has your home ever been bomb damaged? *(Please tick)*
    ☐ Yes   ☐ No

41. Have you ever had a relative, close friend or neighbour seriously injured or killed due to the 'Troubles'? *(Please tick one box for each)*

Relative	☐ Yes	☐ No
Close friend	☐ Yes	☐ No
Neighbour	☐ Yes	☐ No

42. Do you help out a local group (other than church) as a volunteer?
    (Please tick one box)

    No, not at all   Often (at least once a week)
    ☐   ☐   ☐   ☐

43. Have you attended a local community event in the past six months?
    (Please tick one box)

    No, not at all   Yes, several (at least three)
    ☐   ☐   ☐   ☐

44. Are you an active member of a local organisation or club?
    (Please tick one box)

    No, not at all   Yes, very active
    ☐   ☐   ☐   ☐

45. Are you on a management committee or organising committee for any local group or organisation? *(Please tick one box)*

    No, not at all   Yes, several (at least three)
    ☐   ☐   ☐   ☐

46. In the past five year period, have you ever joined a local community action to deal with an emergency? *(Please tick one box)*

    No, not at all   Yes, several times (at least three)
    ☐   ☐   ☐   ☐

47. In the past five year period, have you ever taken part in a local community project? *(Please tick one box)*

    No, not at all   Yes, several times (at least three)
    ☐   ☐   ☐   ☐

Appendix IV The Survey Questionnaire

48. Have you ever been part of a project to organise a new service in your local area (eg youth club, child care, recreation for disabled people)?
    (Please tick one box)

    No, not at all   Yes, several times
    ☐   ☐   ☐   ☐

49. Have you ever picked up other people's rubbish in a public place?
    (Please tick one box)

    No, not at all   Yes, frequently
    ☐   ☐   ☐   ☐

50. If you need information to make a life decision, do you know where to find that information? *(Please tick one box)*

    No, not at all   Yes, definitely
    ☐   ☐   ☐   ☐

51. If you disagreed with what everyone around you agreed on, would you feel free to speak out? *(Please tick one box)*

    No, not at all   Yes, definitely
    ☐   ☐   ☐   ☐

52. If you had a dispute with neighbours (e.g. over fences or dogs), would you be willing to seek mediation? *(Please tick one box)*

    No, not at all   Yes, definitely
    ☐   ☐   ☐   ☐

You and feelings of trust and safety

53. Do you feel safe walking in your neighbourhood after dark?
    (Please tick one box)

    No, not at all   Yes, very much
    ☐   ☐   ☐   ☐

54. Do you agree that most people can be trusted? *(Please tick one box)*

   No, not at all   Yes, very much
   ☐   ☐   ☐   ☐

55. If someone's car breaks down outside your house, do you invite them into your home to use the telephone? *(Please tick one box)*

   No, not at all   Yes, definitely
   ☐   ☐   ☐   ☐

56. Does your area have a reputation for being a safe place? *(Please tick one box)*

   No, not at all   Yes, definitely
   ☐   ☐   ☐   ☐

57. Does your local neighbourhood feel like home? *(Please tick one box)*

   No, not at all   Yes, definitely
   ☐   ☐   ☐   ☐

58. Can you get help from neighbours when you need it? *(Please tick one box)*

   No, not at all   Yes, definitely
   ☐   ☐   ☐   ☐

59. If you were caring for a child and needed to go out for a while, would you ask a neighbour for help? *(Please tick one box)*

   No, not at all   Yes, definitely
   ☐   ☐   ☐   ☐

Appendix IV The Survey Questionnaire

60. Have you visited a neighbour in the past week? *(Please tick one box)*

   No, not at all   Yes, frequently
   ☐   ☐   ☐   ☐

61. When you go shopping in your local area, are you likely to run into friends and acquaintances? *(Please tick one box)*

   No, not at all   Yes, nearly always
   ☐   ☐   ☐   ☐

You and connections with family and friends

---

62. In the past week, how many telephone conversations have you had with friends? *(Please tick one box)*

   None   Many (at least six)
   ☐   ☐   ☐   ☐

63. How many people did you talk to yesterday? *(Please tick one box)*

   None   Many (at least ten)
   ☐   ☐   ☐   ☐

64. Over the weekend, do you have lunch/dinner with people outside your household? *(Please tick one box)*

   No, not usually   Yes, nearly always
   ☐   ☐   ☐   ☐

You and work connections (for those in paid employment)

65. Do you feel part of the local geographical community where you work? *(Please tick one box)*

   No, not at all   Yes, definitely
   ☐   ☐   ☐   ☐

66. Are your work colleagues also your friends? *(Please tick one box)*

   No, not at all   Yes, definitely
   ☐   ☐   ☐   ☐

67. Do you feel part of a team in your place of work? *(Please tick one box)*

   No, not at all   Yes, definitely
   ☐   ☐   ☐   ☐

68. At work, do you take the initiative to do what needs to be done even if no one asks you to? *(Please tick one box)*

   No, not usually   Yes, frequently
   ☐   ☐   ☐   ☐

69. In the past week at work, have you helped a colleague even though it was not in your job description? *(Please tick one box)*

   No, not at all   Yes, several times (at least three)
   ☐   ☐   ☐   ☐

Appendix IV The Survey Questionnaire

You and diversity

---

70. Do you think that the presence of people from a variety of cultural or ethnic groups makes neighbourhood life better? *(Please tick one box)*

    No, not at all   Yes, definitely
    ☐   ☐   ☐   ☐

71. Do you enjoy the idea of living among people of different lifestyles? *(Please tick one box)*

    No, not at all   Yes, definitely
    ☐   ☐   ☐   ☐

72. If a stranger, someone different, moved into your street, would they be accepted by the neighbours? *(Please tick one box)*

    No, not easily   Yes, definitely
    ☐   ☐   ☐   ☐

73. Which of the following groups of people would you prefer not to have as neighbours? *(Please tick all boxes that apply)*

    People with a criminal record   ☐
    People of a different race   ☐
    People of a different religion   ☐
    People with extreme political views   ☐
    People who are heavy drinkers   ☐
    People who are emotionally unstable   ☐
    People who are immigrants   ☐
    People who have AIDS   ☐
    People with a drug addiction   ☐
    People with a homosexual orientation   ☐

You and satisfaction with life

74. Some people feel they have free choice and control over their lives, while others feel that what they do has no real effect on what happens to them. How much freedom and control do you feel you have over the way your life turns out? *(Please tick one box)*

None at all   A great deal
☐   ☐   ☐   ☐

75. Do you feel valued by society? *(Please tick one box)*

No, not much   Yes, very much
☐   ☐   ☐   ☐

76. All things considered, how satisfied are you with your life as a whole these days? *(Please tick one box)*

Not at all satisfied   Very satisfied
☐   ☐   ☐   ☐

77. How often, if at all, do you think about the meaning and purpose of life? *(Please tick one box)*

Often   Sometimes   Rarely   Never
☐   ☐   ☐   ☐

78. Which of the following pair of statements comes closest to your views? *(Please tick one box)*

Humanity has a bright future   ☐

Humanity has a bleak future   ☐

Appendix IV The Survey Questionnaire 193

79. How hopeful are you that it will prove possible to build enough trust to see a stable and peaceful future established for people in Northern Ireland? *(Please tick one box)*

    Not at all hopeful   Very hopeful
    ☐   ☐   ☐   ☐

80. How active do you think the churches should be in trying to improve relations between the communities in Northern Ireland? *(Please tick one box)*

    ☐ Much more active than now   ☐ A little less active than now

    ☐ A little more active than now   ☐ Much less active than now

    ☐ About the same as now   ☐ Don't know

REFERENCES

ACUPA 1985, (Archbishop of Canterbury's Commission on Urban Priority Areas) *Faith in the City: A Call for Action by Church and Nation*. London, Church House Publishing.
Allen Hayes, R. 2001, *Habitat for Humanity: Building Social Capital Through Faith Based Service*. Paper given at the Annual Meeting of the Urban Affairs Association, Detroit, April.
Bacon, D. 1998, *'Splendid and Disappointing': Churches, Voluntary Action and Social Capital in Northern Ireland*. Coleraine, University of Ulster, Centre for Voluntary Action Studies.
Baker, C. 2001, '(Un)Charitable Choice: Religious Organizations Consider Charitable Choice'. *National Housing Institute Shelterforce Online, Jan/Feb*. See http://www.nhi.org/online/issues/115/Baker.html (April 2001).
Baker, J. A. 1981, *The Whole Family of God*. London, Mowbray.
Baron, S., Field, J. & T. Schuller 2000, *Social Capital: Critical Perspectives*. Oxford, Oxford University Press.
Bedford, I. 2002, in a personal communication to the author.
Blair, T. 1999, *Third Sector, Third Way*. Keynote address to annual conference of the National Council for Voluntary Organisations, London, 21st January.
Blair, T. 2001a, *Faith in Politics,* speech to the Christian Socialist Movement, London, 29th March.
Blair, T. 2001b, 'Third Way, phase two'. *Prospect Magazine,* March.
Blunkett, D. 2001, Address to the Churches Main Committee, Westminster Central Hall, London, 19th June.
Boal, F. W., Keane, M. C. & D. N. Livingstone 1997, *Them and Us? Attitudinal Variation Among Churchgoers in Belfast. Belfast,* Institute of Irish Studies.
Bourdieu, P. 1997, 'The Forms of Capital' in Halsey, A. H., Lauder, H., Brown, P. & A. Stuart Wells (eds) *Education: Culture, Economy, Society.* Oxford, Oxford University Press.
Brewer, J. 2002, *Are there any Christians in Northern Ireland?* ARK Seminar presentation, Belfast NICVA, 9/1/02.
Bush, G. W. 2001. See http://www.whitehouse.gov/news/releases/2001/08/unlevelfield.html and http://www.whitehouse.gov/infocus/faith-based/ (September 2001).
Cabinet Office 1999, *Rural Economies*. A Performance and Innovation Unit Report, December. See http://www.cabinet-office.gov.uk/innovation/1999/rural.shtml (August, 2002).
Cabinet Office 2001, *A New Commitment to Neighbourhood Renewal: National*

Strategy Action Plan. Report by the Social Exclusion Unit.
Camden 2000, *Building Bridges Through Faith Communities*. Report by the Office for Public Management, commissioned by the London Borough of Camden.
Cameron, H. 1996, *Unnumbered but not unknown: setting the welfare activities of the local church in a national (UK) context*. Research paper, Centre for Voluntary Organisation, London School of Economics.
Cameron, H. 1998, *The Social Action of the Local Church: Five Congregations in an English City*. PhD thesis, LSE, University of London.
Cameron, H. 2001, 'A perspective from the study of religious organisations' in Anheier, H. (ed) *Organisational theory and the non-profit form*. London, LSE.
Carville, P. J. 1993, *Centenary Book*. Available from Holy Family Presbytery, Newington Avenue, Belfast BT15 2HP.
Catholic Bishops Conference of England and Wales 1996, *The Common Good and the Catholic Church's Social Teaching*. London.
Center for Public Justice 1996, *A Guide to Charitable Choice*. See http://cpjustice.org/Cguide/ccqanda.html (December 2001).
Chaney, P. & R. Fevre 2001, 'Inclusive Governance and "Minority" Groups: The Role of the Third Sector in Wales', in *Voluntas* Vol. 12, Num. 2, June, pp.131-156.
Chaves, M. 1998, 'The Religious Ethic and the Spirit of Nonprofit Entrepreneurship' in Powell W. W. & E. S. Clemens, *Private Action and the Public Good*. New Haven, Yale University Press.
Chester, M., Farrands, M., Finneron, D. & E. Venning 1999, *Flourishing Communities: Engaging church communities with government in New Deal for Communities*. London, Church Urban Fund.
Church Times 2001, 'Chatting quietly about faith', No. 7244, 21/28 December.
Cnaan, R. A. 1998, *Social and Community Involvement of Religious Congregations Housed in Historic Religious Properties: Findings from a Six-City Study*. Final Report to Partners for Sacred Places, University of Pennsylvania.
Cnaan, R. A. 1999, 'Our Hidden Safety Net: Social and Community Work by Urban American Religious Congregations'. *Brookings Review*, Vol. 17, no. 2.
Cnaan, R. A. & S. C. Boddie 2002, 'Charitable choice and faith-based welfare: A call for social work'. *Social Work*, 47 (3), pp. 235-247.
Cnaan, R. A., with Boddie, S. C., Handy, F., Yancey, G. & R. Schneider 2002, *The invisible caring hand: American congregations and the provision of welfare*. New York, New York University Press.
Cnaan, R. A., Wineburg, R. & S. C. Boddie 1999, *The Newer Deal: Social*

Work and Religion in Partnership. New York, Columbia University Press.
Cochrane, F. 2002, *'Bowling Together' within a divided community: Global and local understandings of civil society - the case of Northern Ireland*. Paper presented to the European Consortium for Political research, Turin.
Coleman, J. S. 1990, *Foundations of Social Theory*. Cambridge, Harvard University Press.
Coleman, J. S. 1988, 'Social Capital in the Creation of Human Capital', *American Journal of Sociology*, 94/Supplement: S95-S120.
Cote, S. & Healy, T. 2001, *The Well-being of Nations - The Role of Human and Social Capital*. OECD.
Couto, R. & C. S. Guthrie 1999, *Making Democracy Work Better: Mediating Structures, Social Capital and the Democratic Prospect*. Chapel Hill, NC and London, University of North Carolina Press.
Dasgupta, P. & I. Serageldin (eds) 2000, *Social Capital: A Multicultural Perspective*. Washington DC, World Bank Publications.
Demerath, N. J., Hall, P. D., Schmitt, T. & R. H. Williams (eds) 1998, *Sacred Companies: Organizational Aspects of Religion and Religious Aspects of Organizations*. New York, Oxford University Press.
Department of Social Development 2000, *Consultation Document on Funding for the Voluntary and Community Sector*. Belfast, DSD.
Drummond, T., Simon, E., Williams, M. & L. Anderson 2002, *Neighbourhood Renewal in London: The Role of Faith Communities*. London Churches Group for Social Action and Greater London Enterprise.
DSD 2002, *"How can we effectively address the challenge of weak community infrastructure in Northern Ireland?"* Report of a Department of Social Development Conference held on 10th December 2001.
DSD 2001, *Partners for Change: Government's Strategy for Support of the Voluntary and Community Sector*. Belfast, Department for Social Development, June. See http://www.dsdni.gov.uk/publications/DisplayItemSections.asp?page=1&ID=179 (June 2002).
Education and Training Inspectorate 2002, Report of a General Inspection on National Council of YMCAs. Belfast, Department of Education NI.
Farnell, R., Lund, S., Furbey, R., Lawless, P., Wishart, B. & P. Else 1994, *Hope in the City? The Local Impact of the Church Urban Fund*. Sheffield, Centre for Regional Economic and Social Research, Sheffield Hallam University.
Finding Common Ground: *Recommendations of the Working Group on Human Needs and Faith-Based Community Initiatives*. US Senate, 2002. See

http://www.working-group.org (March 2002).
Fine, B. 2001, *Social Capital versus Social Theory*. London, Routledge.
Finneron, D., Green, L., Harley, S. & J. Robertson 2001, *Challenging Communities: Church Related Community Development and Neighbourhood Renewal.* Durham, Churches Community Work Alliance and Church Urban Fund.
Flint, J. 2001, *The Impact of Church Congregations on Social Capital in Scottish Communities.* Proposal for a Research Collaboration between the Church of Scotland Board of Social Responsibility and the Department of Urban Studies, University of Glasgow.
Focus 2000. Available from Shankill Parish Centre, Church Walk, Lurgan, BT67 9AA.
Foley, M. & B. Edwards 1998, *Is it Time to Disinvest in Social Capital?* Paper given to the American Political Science Meeting. Boston, September.
Forrest, R. & A. Kearns 2001, 'Social Cohesion, Social Capital and the Neighbourhood' in *Urban Studies*, Vol. 38, No. 12, pp. 2125 - 2143.
Fukuyama, F. 1995, *Trust: the Social Virtues and the Creation of Prosperity.* New York, Free Press.
Fulton, J. 1991, *The Tragedy of Belief.* Oxford, Clarendon.
Furbey, R., Else, P., Farnell, R., Lawless, P., Lund, S. & B. Wishart 1997, 'Breaking with Tradition? The Church of England and Community Organising', *Community Development Journal,* Vol. 32, Issue 2, April.
Greeley, A. 1997, 'Coleman Revisited: Religious Structures as a Source of Social Capital', *American Behavioral Scientist*, vol. 40, no. 5.
Grootaert, C. & T. Van Bastelaer 2002, *Understanding and Measuring Social Capital: A Synthesis of Findings and Recommendations from the Social Capital Initiative.* Forum Series on the Role of Institutions in Promoting Economic Growth. See The IRIS Center at http://www.iris.umd.edu/forum/Social%20Capital—final.pdf.
Halpern, D. 1999, *Social Capital: the new golden goose.* Faculty of Social and Political Sciences, Cambridge University.
Halpern, D. 2002, *Social Capital: A Draft Discussion Paper.* Performance and Innovation Unit, March.
Hamilton, N. 2002, *Church and community in North Belfast.* Coleraine, University of Ulster, Centre for Voluntary Action Studies.
Hanifan, L. J. 1916, 'The Rural School Community Center'. *Annals of the American Academy of Political and Social Science* 67:130-138. Quoted in Woolcock, M. & D. Narayan, 'Social Capital: Implications for Development Theory, Research, and Policy. The World Bank Research Observer, vol. 15, no. 2

(August 2000), pp. 225-249.
Harris, M. 1994, *Local religious congregations: what can they contribute to building a civil society?* Paper for ISTR conference, Pecs, Hungary.
Harris, M. 1995, '"Quiet care": welfare work and religious congregations'. *Journal of Social Policy*, vol. 24, no. 1.
Harris, M. 1998, *Organizing God's Work: Challenges for Churches and Synagogues.* London, Macmillan.
Harrison, J. 2000, *Protestant Churches in Areas of Disadvantage: A Series of Case Studies in Belfast.* Belfast Churches' Urban Development Committee.
Harriss, J. 2002, *Depoliticizing Development: The World Bank and Social Capital.* Wimbledon, Anthem Press.
Healy, T. 2002, *The measurement of social capital in a multi-cultural and international context.* Discussion paper for ONS/OECD conference, London, September.
Hickey, J. 1984, *Religion and the Northern Ireland Problem.* Totowa, NJ, Barnes and Noble.
Hirschman, A. O. 1984, 'Against Parsimony: Three Easy Ways of Complicating Some Categories of Economic Discourse'. *American Economic Review*, vol. 74, no. 2, May.
Holy Family Parish Directory 2001. Available from Holy Family Presbytery, Newington Avenue, Belfast BT15, 2HP.
Home Office 1999, *National Strategy for Neighbourhood Renewal: Policy Action Team 9 - Community Self-help.*
Home Office 2000, *National Strategy for Neighbourhood Renewal: Policy Action Team 17 - Joining it up Locally.*
Home Office 2001, *Community Cohesion: A Report of the Independent Review Team (Cantle).* December. See http://www.homeoffice.gov.uk/new_indexs/index_community_cohesion.htm (September 2002).
James, E. 1987, 'The nonprofit sector in comparative perspective', in Powell, W. W. (Ed.), *The nonprofit sector: a research handbook.* New Haven CT, Yale University Press.
Jeavons, T. H. 1998, 'Identifying Characteristics of Religious Organizations', in Demerath et al. 1998.
Kearney, J. & A. Williamson 2001, 'The voluntary and community sector in Northern Ireland: developments since 1995/96', in Etherington, S. & H. Anheier (eds), *Next Steps in Voluntary Action.* London, CCS and NCVO.
Kee, H. C. 1993, *Cambridge Annotated Study Bible.* Cambridge, Cambridge University Press.

References

Kendall, J. 2000, *The mainstreaming of the third sector into public policy in England in the late 1990s: Whys and wherefores.* LSE, Civil Society Working Paper 2.

Kenny, C. (ed.) 1998, *'Imprisoned Within Structures?' The Role of Believing Communities in Building Peace in Ireland (The Believers Enquiry).* Glencree Centre for Reconciliation.

Krishna, A. & E. Shrader 1999, *Social Capital Assessment Tool.* Paper given at the Conference on Social Capital and Poverty Reduction, The World Bank, Washington DC, June.

LGA 2002. *Faith and Community: a good practice guide for local authorities.* Electronic copy available at http://www.lga.gov.uk/Publication.asp?lsection=28&id=SX9D67-A7806AE2 (March 2002).

Liechty, J. & C. Clegg 2001, *Moving Beyond Sectarianism.* Dublin, Columba Press.

McMahon, P. 2001. Address given at the opening ceremony of the Station Centre, Omagh, June.

Messer, J. 1998, 'Agency, Communion and the Formation of Social Capital', *Nonprofit and Voluntary Sector Quarterly,* 27,1.

Morrissey, M. & P. McGinn 2001, *Summary of Interim Report on Research into Evaluating Community-Based and Voluntary Activity in Northern Ireland.* Voluntary Activity Unit, DSD.

Morrow, D. 1995, 'The Protestant churches and social welfare: voluntary action and government support', in Acheson, N. & A. Williamson (eds), *Voluntary Action and Social Policy in Northern Ireland.* Aldershot, Avebury.

Morrow, D., Birrell, D., Greer, J. & T. O'Keefe 1994, *The Churches and Inter Community Relationships.* Coleraine. University of Ulster.

National Statistics Online 2001, *Social Capital Question Bank.* See http://www.statistics.gov.uk/about_ns/social_capital/default.asp (September 2001)

NICVA 2002, *NI Voluntary and Community Sector Almanac,* Belfast.

NI Life and Times 1998. See http://www.ark.ac.uk/nilt/ (July 2002).

NISRA (Northern Ireland Statistics and Research Agency) 2001, *Northern Ireland Census 2001 Key Statistics.* See http://www.nisra.gov.uk/census/Census2001Output/Key%20Statistics/keystatrep.html (December 2002).

Onyx, J. & P. Bullen 1997, *Measuring Social Capital in New South Wales: An Analysis.* Sydney, Centre for Australian Community Organisations and Management, University of Technology, Sydney.

Peake, S. 2001, *A theological reflection on my work.* Unpublished paper.
Pollitt, M. 2000, *Social Capital: an introduction and reflection.* Presentation to East of England Rural Development Agency Churches Network, April.
Portes, A. & P. Landolt 1996, 'The Downside of Social Capital', *The American Prospect* no. 26, May-June.
Putnam, R. D., Leonardi, R. & R. Y. Nanetti 1993, *Making Democracy Work: Civic Traditions in Modern Italy.* Princeton, NJ, Princeton University Press.
Putnam, R. D. 1995, 'Bowling Alone: America's Declining Social Capital', *Journal of Democracy,* 6,1 (January) pp. 65-78.
Putnam, R. D. 1996, 'The Strange Disappearance of Civic America', *The American Prospect,* 24, Winter.
Putnam, R. D. 2000, *Bowling Alone: The collapse and revival of American community.* New York, Simon & Schuster.
Randolph-Horn, E. (ed) 2000, *Faith Makes Communities Work: A report on faith-based community development.* London, Department of the Environment, Transport and the Regions and Shaftesbury.
Richardson, N. 1998, *A Tapestry of Beliefs.* Belfast, Blackstaff Press.
Rossiter, J. 2002, *In the Middle of Our Street: Community Development and the Catholic Church in England and Wales.* A Report from the Catholic Agency for Social Concern. London.
Salt and Pepper 2002, Conference for church based community organisations. East Belfast Mission, April.
Sarkis, A. 2001, *Volunteering Matters - or does it? The role of voluntary action in the 21st century.* Paper presented to the Church Urban Fund, January.
Schneider, J. A. 2001, *Churches, Nonprofits, and Community: The Kenosha Social Capital Study.* Indiana University of Pennsylvania.
Schuller, T. 2000, *The Complementary Roles of Human and Social Capital.* Paper for international symposium on the contribution of human and social capital to sustained economic growth and well-being. Human Resources Development Canada and OECD, Quebec, March.
Sherman, A. L. 2000, *The Growing Impact of Charitable Choice: A Catalogue of New Collaborations Between Government and Faith-based Organizations in Nine States.* Washington, Center for Public Justice.
Skocpol, T. 1996, 'Unravelling From Above', *The American Prospect,* 25, pp. 20-5.
Smith, S. R. & M. R. Sosin 2001. 'The Varieties of Faith-Related Agencies', *Public Administration Review* 61(6): 651-670.
Social Cohesion Network 1997, Policy Research Initiative, Government of Canada.

Sweeney, J. 2001, *From Story to Policy: Social Exclusion, Empowerment and the Churches*. Cambridge, Von Hugel Institute.
Szreter, S. 2000, *A New Political Economy for New Labour: the Importance of Social Capital*. Political Economy Research Centre - University of Sheffield, PERC Policy Paper 15.
Taylor, M. 2002, 'Community and social exclusion' in Nash, V. (ed.) *Reclaiming Community*. London, IPPR, pp. 85-105.
Turley, M. & M. Kavanagh 1990, *Beyond Protest: Reconciliation Through Economic Development*. Dublin, Dominican Publications.
Wells, S. 2002, 'Where locals say what the locality needs', *Church Times*, 7th June.
Wells, S. 2001a, *Generation, Degeneration, Regeneration*. Paper given at the University of East Anglia, Norwich, July.
Wells, S. 2001b, *Ministry on an Urban Estate*. Lecture to the National Readers' Course of the Church of England, August.
Wilkinson, R. 1996, *Unhealthy Societies: The afflictions of inequality*. London, Routledge.
Williamson, A. P. 1995, 'The origins of voluntary action in Belfast,' in Acheson, N. & A. P. Williamson (eds), *Voluntary Action and Social Policy in Northern Ireland*. Aldershot, Avebury.
Williamson, D., Brown, D. & G. Irvine 2001, *dreams judged on delivery*. Belfast, Community Relations Council.
Wineburg, R. J. 2001, *A Limited Partnership: The Politics of Religion, Welfare, and Social Service*. New York, Columbia University Press.
Wineburg, R. J. 1994, 'A Longitudinal Case Study of Religious Congregations in Local Human Services,' *Nonprofit and Voluntary Sector Quarterly*, 23, 2.
Wineburg, R. 1998, Review Carlson-Thies & Skillen (eds), Welfare in America: Christian Perspectives on a Policy in Crisis, *Nonprofit and Voluntary Sector Quarterly*, Vol. 27 No. 1, pp. 98-107.
Wolcott, H. F. 1994 *Transforming Qualitative Data*. Thousand Oaks, Sage.
Woolcock, M. 2000, *The Place of Social Capital in Understanding Social and Economic Outcomes*. Paper prepared for international symposium organized by Human Resources Development Canada and the OECD, Quebec, March.
Woolcock, M. 2002, *Getting the Social Relations Right: Toward an Integrated Theology, Theory, and Strategy of Development Cooperation*. Von Hugel Institute Working Paper WP2002-11, University of Cambridge.
World Bank 2002, Working Papers from the Social Capital Initiative are available at <http://poverty.worldbank.org/library/topic/4294/5050> (August 2002).

World Values Survey. See http://wvs.isr.umich.edu/ (September, 2002).
Wuthnow, R. 1991, *Acts of Compassion.* Princeton, Princeton University Press.
Young, D. R. 1989, 'Local Autonomy in a Franchise Age: Structural Change in National Voluntary Associations'. *Nonprofit and Voluntary Sector Quarterly,* Vol. 18, 2, summer.